Library of Congress Filing Rules

Prepared by John C. Rather and Susan C. Biebel

Processing Services

Library of Congress   Washington   1980

Library of Congress Cataloging in Publication Data

United States. Library of Congress. Processing
     Services.
     Library of Congress filing rules.

     Provisional version by J. C. Rather published in
1971 under title: Filing arrangement in the Library
of Congress catalogs.
     Includes index.
     Supt. of Docs. no.: LC 1.6:F47
     1. Alphabeting.   I.   Rather, John Carson,
1920-   II. Biebel, Susan C. III. Title.
Z695.95.R37 1980   025.3'17   80-607944
ISBN 0-8444-0347-4

Available from the Customer Services Section, Cataloging
Distribution Service, Library of Congress, Washington,
D.C. 20541

PREFACE

In March 1971, the Library of Congress issued new filing rules, Filing Arrangement in the Library of Congress Catalogs, in a provisional version in order to encourage full discussion of its implications for the Library of Congress and to allow for possible changes before its adoption in the Library's catalogs. The provisional version was written by John C. Rather, then specialist in technical processes research at the Library of Congress, and was widely distributed both within the Library of Congress and to other libraries in the United States and abroad. Several computer programs have been written at the Library of Congress to arrange MARC catalog records according to its provisions; it is currently used in the Library's computer-produced bibliographic products. The provisional version was revised by Susan C. Biebel, automation planning specialist, to reflect the experience gained from applying these rules since 1971 and to incorporate the new types of catalog entries in the second edition of the Anglo-American Cataloguing Rules. The publication and adoption of the new Library of Congress Filing Rules in the Library's catalogs in 1981 also means that the previous filing rules, Filing Rules for the Dictionary Catalogs in the Library of Congress (1956), have been superseded by the new filing rules.

TABLE OF CONTENTS

INTRODUCTION

These filing rules have been designed to enable the Library of Congress, with the least possible effort, to arrange large bibliographic files to satisfy a variety of needs. In 1981, simultaneously with the adoption of the second edition of the <u>Anglo-American Cataloguing Rules</u> (AACR 2), the Library of Congress will begin applying these filing rules in its new Add-on Catalog. The adoption of AACR 2 in 1981 implies that only headings formulated according to AACR 2 will be filed in the new card catalog. However, for the immediate future, headings formulated according to earlier cataloging rules will continue to exist in the Library of Congress machine-readable catalog and possibly, for a longer period of time, in catalogs of other libraries. Therefore, these filing rules were written to arrange headings formulated under various cataloging rules and practices. In those situations in which AACR 2 and pre-AACR 2 headings have contradictory characteristics, the filing rules were written to accommodate the new card catalog, which will include only AACR 2 and AACR 2-compatible headings. In those situations in which it may be necessary to write a special rule to arrange forms of headings which cannot occur under AACR 2, the rule has been included in the Appendix because the rule will <u>not</u> be applied by the Library of Congress.

To establish a common understanding of why these rules differ in many respects from those now in the present card catalogs, it may be helpful to explain the assumptions and principles on which they are based.

Assumptions

Seven assumptions were basic to the development of these rules:

1. File arrangement should be hospitable to various kinds of uses: searching for a known item with perfect information; searching for an item with incomplete or inexact information; browsing.

2. Basic rules should be applied consistently with as few exceptions as possible. Consistency has obvious advantages for filers and users, and it facilitates programming for computer filing.

3. Variations in form among name and subject headings are an essential part of the structure of a file arrangement; they should not be ignored in filing. It is illogical to construct a heading one way and then to file it as if it were constructed another way.

4. It is impossible to eliminate all (or even most) filing problems by revising the rules for constructing headings. In a large file, references are required to lead a user from purely formal variations of a heading to the one actually used. Thus, the presence of such references makes it certain that some filing problems will persist regardless of changes in the cataloging rules. In any event, it is possible that headings established under various cataloging rules and practices may coexist in some LC files for an indefinite period.

2

5. The pattern of catalog organization (e.g., dictionary, divided) has an effect on the complexity of arrangement but, in itself, no single pattern can resolve all filing problems. Moreover, the Library of Congress uses alternative patterns for different purposes. Therefore, the rules for filing arrangement should be adaptable to all patterns of catalog organization.

6. Rules for arrangement should discriminate among catalog entries only up to a point. It is unrealistic to expect the rules to provide unique positions for the tiny proportion of entries that would not be differentiated by a standard set of filing fields.

7. The arrangement of the catalog of a large research library cannot be self-explanatory. Its complexity is a function of the number of catalog entries and the diversity of the languages and forms of material represented. When these factors are compounded by efforts to make the catalog responsive to a variety of needs, it is inevitable that the arrangement may be inconvenient or confusing to some users. To alleviate their difficulties, it is imperative to provide a wide range of aids to catalog use. Until this is done, it would be a mistake to suppose that difficulties in using a catalog are attributable solely to defects in its arrangement.

Principles

The foregoing considerations led to the formulation of three basic principles that shaped the development of these rules:

1. Elements in a filing entry should be taken in exactly the form and order in which they appear.

2. Related entries should be kept together if they would be difficult to find when a user did not know their precise form.

3. A standard set of fields should be established for each major type of filing entry.

The first principle emphasizes the way a heading looks, not how it sounds. Similar elements that differ in form (e.g., numbers expressed in digits and those expressed in words) are filed in different positions. The inconvenience of having sometimes to look in two places is outweighed by the fact that no special linguistic knowledge is required to find a numeral or an abbreviation when its printed form is known. These rules allow only a few exceptions to the "file-as-is" principle.

The second principle acknowledges the fact that the more formally constructed a heading is, the less likely a user is to know its elements precisely. Therefore, headings that begin with the same elements are grouped in categories to reduce the time needed to browse in a large file for a heading that is known incompletely.

The third principle applies the legal precept De minimis non curat lex (the law cannot take care of trifles) as a way of preventing the proliferation of special rules. As a result, in some instances (notably certain title main and added entries), the standard set of fields may be insufficient to differentiate among similar filing entries. It seemed unwise, however, to provide for consideration of other information (e.g., place of publication) as a means of further arrangement. Special rules of this kind are difficult to apply either manually or by computer and the nature of the arrangement is frequently not apparent to users. It seemed, therefore, that "no-order" filing was the lesser evil since a desired item could be found by scanning, as is done now when a user lacks full information or does not understand the arrangement or wishes to guard against misfiled entries.

Organization of the Rules

The rules are divided into five parts: 1) a preliminary note that defines the filing terms used in the rules; 2) general rules; 3) special rules; 4) a discussion of aids to catalog use; and 5) an appendix that provides additional information on optional rules to be used in arranging older styles of catalog entries.

The general rules give all of the basic specifications for arranging a file. They are presented systematically, progressing from those of widest applicability to those of more limited scope. Their effect is cumulative so that, to understand any given general rule, one must understand the preceding rules. Each main rule (that is, one with a simple numeral like 3) is subdivided by subordinate numbering (e.g., 3.1, 3.2, 3.2.1) into subrules related to the same aspect of filing arrangement.

Special rules cover particular situations that may be encountered in applying general rules. Although all rules are numbered sequentially, the main special rules are also in alphabetical order by their captions.

These rules have been written to specify what must be done; only rarely do they state what is not to be done. However, examples have been used extensively to show the effect of the rules on types of headings not specifically mentioned in the rules themselves. Whenever possible, the examples were taken directly from the Library of Congress catalogs. Sometimes it has been necessary to make up examples to illustrate the types of filing arrangements that will be created when AACR 2 entries are filed. Although the Add-on Catalog will not include pre-AACR 2 entries, these older forms appear in the examples to illustrate how they would be interfiled in any catalog containing AACR 2 and pre-AACR 2 entries.

Computer Filing

The ability to arrange bibliographic entries by computer in an efficient manner depends on a consistent set of rules for arrangement, a machine-readable format that affords adequate identification of key elements in a catalog record, and a flexible program for building sort keys that can be used in sorting or arranging catalog records. These components of a machine filing system are so closely interrelated, however, that it is not easy to assess their relative importance.

The present rules have been designed to satisfy the first requirement. Although the primary concern was to obtain arrangements that are relatively easy for humans to achieve and to use, the final test of the practicality of a rule was whether a computer could be programmed to apply it efficiently. Clearly it was not possible to make such a decision without considering the other basic components of a machine filing system. This was done by taking account of the content designators (tags, indicators, subfield codes) in the MARC format and the capabilities of the LIBSKED (Library Sort Key Edit) program developed by the Library.

The LIBSKED program is now used, on a regular basis, to arrange MARC records to produce the following Library of Congress bibliographic products: Audiovisual Materials, Library of Congress Subject Headings, and the microform edition of Name Authorities. Another set of programs based on LIBSKED is used to arrange MARC records for the Library's online retrieval system, the MUMS Search Service. The experience gained during the development of these two programs and from the users of the resulting products has been helpful in identifying the areas of the provisional version that needed revision.

The close relationship of filing rules to the other components of a machine retrieval system was clearly demonstrated during the development of the online filing programs. Recognition of this fact leads to the following corollary which should be considered by anyone responsible for the design or construction of an online retrieval system:

The treatment of bibliographic data specified by these filing rules should also apply in the construction of search queries and the display of brief records retrieved.

The reason for this corollary is fairly obvious. It is much easier for a user to comprehend an online retrieval system if the data is treated consistently by the various system components. For example, if a hyphenated word is considered as two words by the filing rules, it should be considered as two words whenever a title key is constructed using the hyphenated word. Or, if an author-title key is constructed using an added entry and bibliographic title, the same added entry and bibliographic title fields should be used to arrange the record and these fields should be prominently displayed when the brief record is displayed.

PRELIMINARY NOTE ON FILING TERMS

The following glossary of terms used in this document will be helpful in understanding the specifications for filing arrangement. Although the terms and their definitions differ somewhat from those commonly used in discussing the arrangement of catalog entries, they are intended to permit clear, consistent presentation of the rules.

Filing Entry: All the fields that may be considered in determining the filing position of an item in a catalog; for example, a name heading, title, and publication date.

Field: A major component of a filing entry that comprises one or more elements (e.g., a heading; a title).

Element: One or more words that make up an integral part of a field (e.g., the surname in a personal name heading). An element and a field are are identical when the field contains only one element; for example, a title. The first element in a field is called the leading element; the others are called subordinate elements. For example, in the personal name heading, Carpenter, William, 1871-1944, the leading element is Carpenter; while William and 1871-1944 are subordinate elements.

Word: One or more characters set off by spaces and/or marks of significant punctuation.

Character: A letter, digit, symbol, or mark of punctuation. In a machine record, a space is a character.

9

Significant Punctuation: A mark of punctuation that indicates the end of an element. Typical cases include: 1) the period after a direct order corporate name, e.g., Yale University. Library; 2) the comma after a surname, e.g., Johnson, Edgar; 3) parentheses indicating an addition to a place name, e.g., Florence (Italy); 4) the colon separating date and place in a conference heading, e.g., Conference on Cancer Public Education (1973 : Dulles Airport).

Punctuation that does not indicate the end of an element is considered nonsignificant. Common instances include: 1) a period after an abbreviation, e.g., Mr.; 2) a comma to increase readability (as in 10,000,000 or Smith, Kline, and French Laboratories). Although nonsignificant punctuation is generally ignored in filing, it may require special treatment in certain situations, e.g., hyphenation, decimals.

Components of a filing entry

Filing entry

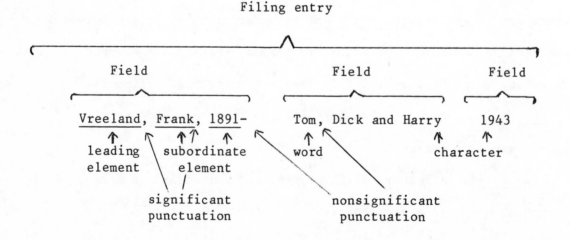

GENERAL RULES

1.   <u>Basic Filing Order</u>

Fields in a filing entry are arranged word by word, and words are arranged character by character. This procedure is continued until one of the following occurs:

   a. A prescribed filing position is reached.

   b. The field comes to an end (in which case placement is determined by another field of the entry or by applying one of the rules given hereafter).

   c. A mark of punctuation indicating a subarrangement is encountered.

1.1.   Order of Letters

Letters are arranged according to the order of the English alphabet (A-Z). Upper and lower case letters have equal filing value.

1.1.1   Modified Letters

Modified letters are treated like their plain equivalents in the English alphabet. Thus all diacritical marks and modifications of recognizable English letters are treated as if they did not exist; e.g., ä, á, å, ł, ñ, ø are filed as a, 1, n, o. The treatment of special letters that cannot be readily equated with English letters is described in Rule 17.

Example

    Hand blows
    Hand book for Prospect Park
    Hand in glove
    Håndbok for sangere
    Handbook for adventure
    Hände am Pflug
    Hands on the past
    Haṇḍu   [Indic surname]

1.2.   Placement of Numerals

Numbers expressed in digits or other notation (e.g., roman numerals) precede letters and, with few exceptions, they are arranged according to their numerical value. According to this rule, all filing entries beginning with numerals appear before entries beginning with the letter A. Numbers expressed as words are filed alphabetically. Detailed instructions for filing numerals are given in Rule 16.

Example

    1, 2, 3, and more
    1, 2, buckle my shoe
    3 died variously
    10 ways to become rich
    13 jolly saints
    112 Elm Street
    838 ways to amuse a child
    1000 spare time money making ideas
    1984
    10,000 trade names
    1,000,000 delinquents
    A is for anatomy
    A4D desert speed run
    Aa, Abraham
    Henry II
    Henry 3
    Henry VIII and his six wives

```
Henry Street Settlement, New York
Henry the Fourth, part two
Longitude 30 west
Longitude and time
Nineteen eighty-four
Oberlin College
One, two, three for fun
Rubinstein, Moshe F.
Ten thousand miles on a bicycle
Three 14th century English mystics
Three by Tey
Thucydides
```

1.3.   Signs and Symbols

Nonalphabetic signs and symbols within a field are generally ignored in filing and the remaining letters or numerals are used as the basis of arrangement (see also Rule 18).

1.3.1.   Punctuation

Punctuation as such has no place in the collating sequence of characters considered in filing arrangement. A mark of punctuation is taken into account, however, in two situations: 1) when it signals the end of an element or field and indicates the need for subarrangement as described in the following rules; and 2) when it serves as the sole separator between two discrete words (e.g., Mott-Smith; 1951/1952; 1:3) and so must be treated as equivalent to a space. The second situation dictates that a hyphen will always be treated as a space (see also Rules 12 and 16).

2.   Significant Filing Elements

Elements in a field are taken exactly as they appear with few exceptions. Thus, the position of a filing entry is basically determined by the order and form of the fields it contains. In some cases, however, the filing form of an element may differ from the bibliographic form for one or more of the following reasons:

a. A word may be omitted (e.g., an initial article in a bibliographic title field).

b. A word may be expanded (e.g., the period subdivision "To 1500" is filed as "0—1500").

c. A word may be added (e.g., bracketed information is added to the title proper to describe a symbol which cannot be printed by the available typography).

d. A word may be relocated (e.g., Ward, Mrs. Humphry is arranged as if it were Ward, Humphry, Mrs.).[1]

Treatment of specific situations is described in later rules.

[1]The Library of Congress will continue its present practice of placing terms of honor and address after a person's forename. Therefore, it will not be necessary to apply Rule 2.d. at the present time at the Library of Congress.

3.   Identification of Elements in a Field

Elements in a field containing more than one element are generally indicated by a dash, period, comma, colon, or parenthesis. This
rule does not apply when these marks of punctuation are not significant
(Rule 3.1) or under the conditions described in Rule 3.2.1.

3.1.   Nonsignificant Punctuation in a Field

A field may contain a dash, period, comma, colon, or parenthesis that does not indicate the end of an element. For example, a dash
in a title (e.g., Birds--their life, their ways, their world); a period
after an abbreviation (e.g., St. Louis); commas used to separate words
in a series (e.g., Sears, Roebuck and Company); a colon in a conference
name (e.g., Symposium: Care of the Professional Voice); parentheses to
set off a word within a name (e.g., Vickers (Aviation) Limited). The
following guidelines may be helpful in discriminating between significant and nonsignificant punctuation: 1) significant punctuation indicates a formal combination of elements in a field, often with the
punctuation being added by the cataloger according to prescribed rules;
2) nonsignificant punctuation occurs as an integral part of a name or
title.

3.2.   Leading Element

The leading element in a field is indicated by the first significant dash, period, comma, colon, or parenthesis, except when the
field contains a forename followed by a roman numeral (Rule 3.2.1).

3.2.1.   Forenames with Numeration

When a forename is followed by a roman numeral (as in a heading
for a pope or sovereign), the leading element ends before the numeral.

3.3.   Leading Elements in Various Types of Fields

In the following sections, examples of leading elements in
various types of fields are shown by underlining. Within each field
type, the examples are grouped according to the punctuation mark which
determines the end of the leading element. The punctuation mark is indicated in the left-hand margin. Bear in mind that these examples are not
intended to illustrate filing arrays which are covered by later rules.

3.3.1.   Personal Name Fields

In addition to fields beginning with a forename or a surname,
personal name fields include cases where entry is made under the distinguishing word in a nobleman's title, the name of a bishop's see, initials, letters, numerals, phrases, or the name of a family, clan,
dynasty, house, or other such group.

Examples

a. Forenames

Charles the Great
Plato

Comma

Charles, Prince of Wales, 1948–
John, the Baptist
John of the Cross, Saint, 1542–1591
Joseph Aloysius, Father, O.M.I.
Leonardo, da Vinci, 1452–1519
Moses ben Jacob, of Coucy, 13th cent.

Dash

Plato--Biography

Parenthesis

Abraham (Patriarch)
Prachākitkǫračhak (Chǣm), Phrayā

Period

Aristoteles. Spurious and doubtful works
Plato. Republic

Blank
(Rule 3.2.1.)

Charles XIV John, King of Sweden and Norway, 1763–1844
John XXIII, Pope, 1881–1963
Victor Emmanuel II, King of Italy, 1820–1878

b. Surnames

Comma

Byron, George Gordon Byron, Baron, 1788–1824
Canterbury, William Wake, Abp. of   [reference]
Cobo de Rumazo Gonzáles, Inés, 1906–1974
Du Maurier, Daphne, Dame, 1907–
Essex, Robert Devereux, Earl of, 1566–1601
Eximio, Dr.
O'Connor, Jane
Rodríguez H., Guadalupe (Rodríguez Hernández)
Smith, Russell E. (Russell Edgar)
Smith-Hinds, William L., 1938–
Trịnh, Vân Thanh

c. Initials, Letters, Numerals, Phrases

<u>110908</u>
<u>A. De O.</u>
<u>Author of Early impressions</u>
<u>Mr. Fixit</u>

Comma   <u>i. e.</u>, Master
                     <u>Memoirs of a fox-hunting man</u>, Author of   [reference]
                     <u>Richard</u>, Poor
                     <u>S.</u>, D., Master   [reference]

Dash   <u>Dr. X</u>—Bibliography

Parenthesis   <u>Espirito Universal</u> (Spirit)
                     <u>H. D.</u> (Hilda Doolittle), 1886-1961

d. Family Names

                     <u>Brown family</u>
Dash   <u>Brown family</u>—Periodicals
Parenthesis   <u>Brown family</u> (Chad Brown, d. 1665?)
Comma   <u>Hapsburg</u>, House of

3.3.2.   Place and Corporate Name Fields

In the following examples, place name fields and corporate name fields are treated together because a corporate name field may begin with the name of a place. The examples also include instances of nonsignificant punctuation.

<u>Examples</u>

<u>Bender (Matthew) and Company, inc.</u>
<u>George Washington University</u>, Washington, D. C.

India
Larousse, firm, publishers, Paris
Mathematica, Inc.
Miami, University of, Coral Gables, Fla.
St. Louis Metropolitan Area Airport Authority
University of California, Los Angeles
University of Wisconsin--Madison
Wilson, H. W., firm, publishers

Comma

Germany, West
ICU Symposium on Sociolinguistics, 1st, Tokyo, 1974
Quezon, Philippines

Dash

Center for Disease Control--Juvenile literature
France--Commerce--History

Parenthesis

Amsterdam (Netherlands)
Apollo II (Spacecraft)
Cyprus (Archdiocese)
Newman Club (Brooklyn College)
Northeast Agricultural Leadership Assembly (1979 :
    Cherry Hill, N.J.)
Sociedad Nacional de Minería (Peru)
St. Augustine (Fla.)
Systems, Science and Software (Firm)
Washington University (St. Louis, Mo.)

Period

American Bar Association. Section of International Law
India. Parliament
Paris. Peace Conference, 1919
St. Louis University. Metropolitan College

3.3.3. Uniform Title Fields

Uniform titles occur in the following situations: 1) interposed
between a heading and a bibliographic title; 2) used as a heading; 3) used
as the title portion of a heading consisting of a name-title combination.
All are treated in the same way for the purpose of determining elements.

19

Martin Chuzzlewit
Mass, Sainte Thérèse
Piano music, 4 hands
Violin, piano music

Comma   Canzonets, voices (4)
Symphonies, D. 589, C major
Trios, flute, clarinet, bassoon
Works, organ. Selections

Dash   Bible--Astronomy

Parenthesis   Genesis (Anglo-Saxon poem)
Good farming (Eastern edition)
Goyescas (Piano work)
Journal of education (Easton, Pa.)
Life (Chicago)
Liturgy of the hours (U.S.)
Le sacre du printemps (Sketches)
Treaty of Paris (1763)

Period   Aïda. Celeste Aïda
Babar en famille. English. Sound recording
Bible. N.T. Epistles of John. Polyglot
Gone with the wind. [Motion picture]
Iliad. Book 1. English
Treaties, etc. Great Britain

Semicolon   Le corsaire; arr.
Lamb research report ; no. 3

3.3.4.   Bibliographic Title Fields

The filing entry for bibliographic titles is the title proper;
usually it consists of a single element. For the purpose of determining elements, series statements are considered bibliographic titles. In
determining the leading element, punctuation within the title proper is

disregarded, unless the name of a part/section or series numeration is present. Title added entries are supplied in the required form prior to filing. When a work is entered under title, however, the filer must determine the end of the title proper. It usually occurs at the first mark of punctuation but the sense of the title may require that it be extended beyond that point. If the title was cataloged using ISBD punctuation, the different data elements are indicated by different marks of punctuation.

Examples

The D.O.D. Joint Parachute Test Facility
Dangerous cargo--accepting and airlifting
The listing attic ; The unstrung harp 1/
Oswald Spengler, a critical estimate
Sonate en ré majeur, opus 3, pour violon
Under the hill, or, The story of Venus and
    Tannhaüser 1/

Bracket   All that jazz [motion picture]

Colon   Human life : our legacy and our challenge / general
                   editor ...
               India's great son : Soviet people about Nehru / com-
                   piled and ...

Comma   A Chinaman in my bath, and other pieces, by Lord
                   Mancroft

1/According to AACR 2, the title proper may include multiple titles if an item lacks a collective title or if an alternative title is present. Because the punctuation for these titles is not always sufficient to clearly designate the first title, the leading element is defined as the complete title proper. The cataloger will provide variant title added entries for each title represented in the title proper, as appropriate.

Period	Addition and subtraction. [Transparencies] Addition: commutative and associative. [Transparencies] Addition-subtraction-regrouping of whole numbers. [Transparencies] Cuando yo sea grande (When I grow up). [Motion picture] Faust. Part one Key abstracts. Industrial power and control systems Progress in nuclear energy. Series 2, Reactors
Semicolon	Yesterday's clowns; the rise of film comedy.
Slash	Chicano voices / [edited by] Carlota ... Human life cycle / edited by ...

3.3.5.   Topical Subject Heading Fields

The following examples show the leading elements of various types of topical subject headings and also illustrate cases of nonsignificant punctuation. In topical subject headings, a comma followed by an upper-case letter is significant. When the following letter is lower-case, the comma is nonsignificant.

Examples

Amblyopia
Gothic-roman type controversy
Hotels, taverns, etc., in literature
Piano, flute, viola with string orchestra
World War, 1939-1945

Comma	Death, Apparent Debt, Imprisonment for (Jewish law) Forestry law and legislation, Colonial Gothenburg, Sweden, in literature Government, Resistance to, in literature Lasers, Effect of radiation on Necessity, Fort, Battle of, 1754 Wagner, Richard, 1813-1883, in fiction, drama, poetry, etc.

22

Dash   Death--Causes
                        Government business enterprises--Accounting
                        Hotels, taverns, etc.--Austria

Parenthesis   Charitable uses, trusts, and foundations (Hindu law)
                        Death (African religion)
                        Paris (France) in literature
                        Piano (1 hand) with orchestra
                        Violins (2), viola with orchestra
                        Wheels (in religion, folk-lore, etc.)

4.   Order of Fields with Identical Leading Elements

Fields with identical leading elements are grouped together.
When the leading elements in a group represent different types of enti-
ties, the order of arrangement is as follows:

    a. Person: (1) Forename

                (2) Surname

    b. Place

    c. Thing: (1) Corporate body

                (2) Topical subject heading

    d. Title
             [Uniform titles and bibliographic
             titles are interfiled]

Example

      George III, King of Great Britain, 1738-1820
      George, Saint, d. 303
      George, Alan
      George, William C.
      George (Ariz.)
      George (Motor boat)   [corporate body]
      George, Lake, Battle of, 1755   [subject heading]
      George [motion picture]

4.1.   Placement of Certain Categories of Leading Elements

For the purpose of file arrangement, personal names of the following types, which are entered in direct order, are considered to be
forenames: 1) a name consisting entirely or primarily of initials,
separate letters or numerals; 2) a name consisting of a phrase or
other appellation that is not a real name. If the two types of names

described above are not present in direct order, the leading element is considered to be a surname. Leading elements of the following types are also considered to be surnames: 1) the distinguishing word in a nobleman's title; 2) the name of a bishop's see; 3) the name of a family, clan, dynasty, house, or other such group. If a corporate body is entered under the name of a jurisdiction, the leading element is considered to be a place. If the heading for a manuscript or manuscript group begins with the heading of a corporate body, the leading element is considered to be a corporate body.

Examples

Forenames: 110908
Author of Early impressions
D. S., Master
Father Time

Surnames: Bolingbroke, Henry St. John, Viscount, 1618-1751
Other, A. N.
Windsor, House of

Place: Canada. Canadian Army

Corporate body: British Library. Manuscript. Arundel 384

5. <u>Order of Subordinate Filing Elements</u>

When the leading elements of two or more fields are identical and they represent the same type of entity, the arrangement takes account of subordinate filing elements according to the following patterns. The position of a leading element followed by more than one subordinate element is determined by the order in which the elements appear.

5.1. Forename Fields

The leading element of a forename field may be followed by one or more of the following categories of subordinate elements: 1) numeration; 2) dates; 3) additional words. When forename fields have identical leading elements, they are grouped in the following order:

    a. Forename alone

    b. Forename with numeration   ⎤ filed in one numerical sequence
       Forename, date(s)   ⎦

    c. Forename, additional word(s)

Additional words may include titles, a characterizing word or phrase, and the full form of initials used in the name. In arranging additional words within a group, differences in punctuation are ignored.

    <u>Examples</u>

        Charles
        Charles II, King of Great Britain, 1630-1685
        Charles III, King of Navarre, 1361-1425
        Charles XIV John, King of Sweden and Norway, 1763-1844
        Charles, 13th cent.   [made-up] [files as 1200-1299]

```
Charles (Anglo-Norman poet)    [made-up]
Charles, Count of Flanders, d. 1127
Charles, espírito
Charles, Prince of Wales, 1948-
Charles (Writer)               [made-up]
Charles the Great              [reference]

Richard, 1928-
Richard, of St. Victor, d. 1173
Richard, Poor                  [forename]
Richard, Carolle               [surname]
Richard Alfred, 1932-          [compound forename]
```

5.2.   Surname Fields

The leading element of a surname field (as defined in Rule 4.1)
may be followed by one or more of the following categories of subordinate
elements: 1) forenames, initials, or (in the case of a nobleman, bishop,
or family) a full name; 2) dates; 3) additional words; 4) a relator.
Additional words may include terms of honor and address, characterizing
words or phrases, and the full form of initials used in the name. A
relator is a word that shows the function of a name in relation to a work
with which the name is associated [in general not used under AACR 2].
Further information on the treatment of relators is found in Rule 11.3.
When surname fields with identical leading elements have subordinate elements in the first three categories, they are grouped in the following
order:

    a. Surname alone
    b. Surname, date(s)
    c. Surname, additional word(s)
    d. Surname, forename
    e. Surname, forename, date(s)
    f. Surname, forename, additional word(s)

<u>Examples</u>

```
Smith
Smith, fl. 1641
Smith, Mrs.
Smith (Name)
Smith, Alan, 1925-
Smith, Alan, 1925- (Spirit)              [made-up]
Smith, G. C.
Smith, G. C. (Gordon C.)
Smith, G. Louis, 1900-                   [made-up]
Smith, G. Louis (George Louis)
Smith, G. Louis (Glen Louis)             [made-up]
Smith, G. R.
Smith, George, 1845-1918
Smith, George A.
Smith, Graham, 1942-
Smith, Graham, Solicitor
Smith, Graham O.
Smith-Durland, Eugenia, 1935-
Smith family
Smith-Magowan, David

Windsor, House of
Windsor, Arthur Lloyd
```

5.3.   Place Name Fields

When the leading elements of two or more place name fields or place names at the beginning of corporate name fields are identical, the fields are grouped in the following order:

a. Place name alone

b. Place name followed by parenthetical qualifier

c. Place name followed by comma and additional words

Subarrangement within any group is by succeeding subordinate elements.

Subordinate elements are generally indicated by colons, parentheses or

periods. The third group (place names with significant commas) will not

occur in AACR 2 place name fields.

Examples

```
        Cambridge.  University.  Board of Graduate Studies
        Cambridge.  University.  Emmanuel College.  Chapel
        Cambridge.  University.  King's College
        Cambridge (Cambridgeshire)
        Cambridge (Mass.)
        Cambridge (Mass.).  City Council
        Cambridge, Eng.  Environment Committee
        Cambridge, Eng.  Kettle's Yard Gallery         [reference]
        Cambridge, Ont.
        Cambridge Apostles (Society)
        Cambridge Historical Commission
        Cambridge Legal History Conference, 1975

        United States.  91st Congress, 2d session, 1970.  Senate
        United States.  94th Congress, 1st session, 1975
        United States.  Army.  General Staff
        United States.  Aviation Forecast Branch
        United States.  Congress (87th : 1961-1962).  House
        United States.  Congress (87th, 2nd session : 1962)
        United States.  President (1909-1913 : Taft)
        United States.  President, 1913-1921 (Wilson)
        United States.  President (1933-1945 : Roosevelt)
        United States.  President, 1953-1961 (Eisenhower)

        New York (City).  Police Dept.
        New York (City).  Stock Exchange
        New York (N.Y.).  Dept. of Water Resources
        New York (N.Y.).  Environmental Protection Administration
        New York (State).  Dept. of Commerce
        New York (State).  Office of Health Systems Management
```

5.4.   Corporate Name Fields

When the leading elements of two or more corporate name fields
are identical, the fields are grouped in the following order:

a. Corporate name alone

b. Corporate name followed by parenthetical qualifier

Subarrangement within any group is by succeeding subordinate elements.

Examples

Symposium on Oil Shale
Symposium on Oil Shale (10th : 1977 : Colorado School of
    Mines)
Symposium on Oil Shale (12th : 1979 : Colorado School of
    Mines)
Symposium on Oil Shale, 8th, Colorado School of Mines,
    1975 1/
Symposium on Oil Shale, 9th, Colorado School of Mines,
    1976 1/
Symposium on Optimization, Nice, 1969
Symposium on Optimization, Toronto, 1968

University of Alaska (College)   [reference]
University of Alaska (System). Cooperative Extension
    Service
University of Alaska, Anchorage. Criminal Justice Center
University of Alaska, Anchorage. Library
University of Alaska Art Fair   [made-up]
University of Alaska, Fairbanks. Institute of Marine
    Science
University of Alaska, Juneau

1/As a result of the basic punctuation patterns in AACR 2 corporate headings, Rule 3.3.2 treats the comma in corporate headings as not significant. Consequently, this example shows corporate names with commas following corporate names with parentheses. In actuality, the LC online
retrieval system does not recognize this difference in punctuation for
conferences and it will arrange the conference headings in numerical
order--8, 9, 10, 12.

5.5.   Uniform Title Fields

         When the leading elements of two or more uniform title fields

are identical but one heading is not qualified and the others are, the

fields are grouped in the following order:

         a.   Uniform title alone

         b.   Uniform title followed by parenthetical qualifier

         Examples

                 Contact!
                 Contact (Kansas City, Mo.)   [reference]
                 Contact (Montréal, Québec)
                 Contact (Real Estate Institute of Canada)
                 Contact (Toronto Nutrition Committee)
                 Contact (Waterloo, Ont.)
                 Contact (World Federalist Youth)
                 Contact and change

                 The twentieth century
                 The Twentieth century (Filmstrip)
                 The Twentieth century (London, England)
                 The Twentieth century (Television program)

5.5.1.   Subordinate Elements of Uniform Titles

         The subordinate elements of a uniform title heading or a uniform

title associated with a name heading may include terms describing 1) a

part of the larger work (including form subheadings such as "selections");

2) language of the text; 3) name of the version; 4) date associated with

the text; 5) other parties in a treaty heading; and 6) qualifying words.

When different types of subordinate elements occur in the same relative

position (for example, as the second element), the fields are grouped in

the following order:

a. Date

b. Language

c. All other subordinate elements, except qualifying words

d. Qualifying words

<u>Examples</u>

```
Bible.  English.  1808.  Thomson
Bible.  English.  1898.  Revised
Bible.  English.  1966.  Jerusalem Bible
Bible.  English.  Authorized.  1976
Bible.  English.  Authorized.  Selections.  1980
Bible.  English.  Harmonies.  1842.  Authorized
Bible.  English.  New American.  Selections.  1973
Bible.  English.  New American Standard.  1971
Bible.  English.  Selections.  1966.  Authorized
Bible.  Latin.  King Sancho's Bible
Bible.  Latin.  Selections.  1974
Bible.  Latin.  Vulgate.  1975
Bible.  Spanish.  Selections.  1971
Bible.  N.T.  James.  Latin.  1913
Bible.  O.T.  English.  1952.  New American
Bible.  O.T.  Spanish.  Selections.  1974
Bible.  O.T.  Exodus.  English.  Childs.  1974
Bible.  O.T.  Psalms.  English.  Selections.  1976
Bible.  O.T.  Psalms.  Latin.  Romana.  1965
The Bible (Motion picture)
The Bible and archaeology
```

<u>Hypothetical example for a group of uniform titles with an identical main entry</u>

```
United States
    [Treaties, etc.  1984 Nov. 18]
    [Treaties, etc.  1987 May 18]
    [Treaties, etc.  Afghanistan, 1982 May 24]
    [Treaties, etc.  Afghanistan, 1982 June 26]
    [Treaties, etc.  Brazil, 1971 Apr. 2]
    [Treaties, etc.  Canada, 1970 Aug. 12]
```

Additional instructions for arranging uniform titles are given in Rule 19.

5.6.   Bibliographic Title Fields

Bibliographic title fields include series statements. The leading element of a bibliographic title may be followed by one or more of the following categories of subordinate elements: 1) number of a part/section; 2) name of a part/section; 3) series ISSN; 4) series or volume number. Bibliographic title fields with identical leading elements are grouped in the following order:

a. Bibliographic title alone

b. Bibliographic title followed by name or number of part/section

Subarrangement within any group is by succeeding subordinate elements.

Examples

```
Focus
Focus.  Biology
Focus.  Black American bibliography series
Focus.  Teaching English language arts
Focus.  Urban society
Focus (Television program)          [made-up uniform title]
Focus Education, inc.
Focus for the future
Focus on America--the Northeast region ; no. 1
Focus on America--the Northeast region ; no. 3

Journal of polymer science.  Part A, General papers
Journal of polymer science.  Part A-1:  Polymer chemistry
Journal of polymer science.  Part A-2.  Polymer physics
Journal of polymer science.  Part B.  Polymer letters
Journal of polymer science.  Part C.  Polymer symposia
   no. 14
Journal of polymer science.  Part C.  Polymer symposia
   no. 18
```

5.7.   Topical Subject Headings

When the leading elements of two or more topical subject headings are identical but they are distinguished by different means, the
fields are grouped in the following order:

       a. Leading element alone

       b. Leading element followed by a dash and subject subdivi-
           sion(s)

       c. Leading element followed by a comma and additional word(s)

       d. Leading element followed by parenthetical qualifier

Subarrangement within any group is by succeeding subordinate elements.

      <u>Example</u>

```
Children
Children--Surgery
Children, Adopted
Children, Vagrant
Children (International law)
Children (Roman law)
Children as authors
```

5.8.   Subject Subdivisions

In any subject heading field, subordinate elements that follow
a dash (that is, subject subdivisions) are grouped in the following order:

       a. Period subdivisions

       b. Form and topical subdivisions

       c. Geographical subdivisions

These distinctions are maintained at every level of subject subdivision.
The treatment of subject subdivisions in relation to other subdivisions
of the same heading is described in Rule 7.2.

Examples

German literature   [see-also reference]
German literature--18th century
German literature--20th century
German literature--Addresses, essays, lectures
German literature--Catholic authors
German literature--Style
German literature--Bavaria
German literature--Switzerland
German literature in foreign countries

Catholic Church--Government
Catholic Church--History--16th century
Catholic Church--History--20th century
Catholic Church--History--1965-
Catholic Church--History--Juvenile literature
Catholic Church--History--Sources
Catholic Church--Hymns

6.   Functional Order of Fields

When the first fields of two or more filing entries are identical and the fields represent the same entity, the entries are grouped
according to the cataloging function of these fields (that is, their
relationship to the work cataloged or their use in the catalog). In general, filing entries can be considered as either headings associated with
a bibliographic record or headings associated with an authority record.
A bibliographic record contains the main entry assigned to a work, added
entries including series entries, and subject entries. An authority record may contain the information needed to generate any of the following
cards or references: 1) an authority card for an established name or
subject heading; 2) a linking reference from the new form of name established according to AACR 2 to the form of name used in the Old Catalog;
3) an explanatory reference which provides information relating to searching and filing arrangement; 4) an information or history card on the different forms of name associated with an entity; 5) a see reference from a
non-established name to one or more established headings; 6) a see-also
reference from one established heading to one or more established headings. Filing entries for bibliographic records and authority records are
grouped in the following order:

<u>Names</u>

    a. Authority card for an established name or subject heading
    b. Linking reference from a name heading
    c. Explanatory reference, information card, see reference from
        a name
    d. See-also reference from a name
    e. Main entry, added entry for bibliographic records

<u>Subjects</u>

    f. Explanatory reference, information card, see reference from
        a subject
    g. See-also reference from a subject
    h. Subject entries for bibliographic records

Note that the order shown above specifies that all main and added entries

for bibliographic records are interfiled.

<u>Examples</u>

```
Canada.  Armed Forces          [authority card]
Canada.  Armed Forces          [information card]
  An act came into force on...
Canada.  Armed Forces          [main entry]
  Badges of the Canadian Forces
CANADA.  ARMED FORCES          [subject entry]


Gaulle, Charles de, 1890-1970 [authority card]
Gaulle, Charles de, 1890-1970
  Search also under
    France.  President (1959-1969 : De Gaulle)
Gaulle, Charles de, 1890-1970    [main entry]
  Memoirs of hope
GAULLE, CHARLES DE, 1890-1970
  Search also under
    POSTAGE-STAMPS--TOPICS--GAULLE, CHARLES DE, 1890-1970
GAULLE, CHARLES DE, 1890-1970--ANECDOTES


Saint Louis Museum of Fine Arts          [authority card]
Saint Louis Museum of Fine Arts          [linking reference]
  For works cataloged before 1981 search
  in the old catalog under
    Washington University, St. Louis.  Saint Louis Museum
    of Fine Arts
```

7.   Placement of Certain Types of Fields

To obtain coherent groupings of filing entries relating to the same entity, the following rules must be observed in arranging three types of fields: 1) name-title fields; 2) fields containing subject subdivisions; 3) subject entries for uniform title fields.

7.1.   Name-Title Fields

A field comprising a personal or corporate name heading and a uniform title (e.g., Homerus. Odyssea; Marga Institute. Marga research studies ; 5) is treated as if it consisted of two separate fields containing the same information. Thus, with respect to this consideration, no distinction is made between a filing entry containing separate fields for a name heading and a title and a filing entry containing a name-title added or subject entry for the same work. See Rule 8 for instruction on the arrangement of entries under the name of a personal or corporate body.

7.2.   Fields Containing Subject Subdivisions

A field containing a subject subdivision is treated as if it consisted of at least two parts: the heading proper and the subject subdivision(s). In the case of name-title fields with subject subdivisions, the field is treated as if it consisted of three parts (name, title, subject subdivision) to satisfy the requirements of Rule 7.1. In both

circumstances, the subject heading field is grouped with main and added
entry fields containing the heading proper. After the functional order
of the fields has been taken into account (see Rule 6), arrangement is by
subject subdivision.

Examples

```
Homerus
   Ilias.  Armenian
Homerus
   Odyssea
Homerus.  Odyssea            [name-title added entry]
HOMERUS.  ODYSSEA            [name-title subject entry]
HOMERUS.  ODYSSEA--ILLUSTRATIONS
Homerus.  Paraphrases, tales, etc. 1/
Homerus
   Poetica e poesia
Homerus.  Spurious and doubtful works 1/
HOMERUS
HOMERUS--APPRECIATION


Canada                                      [main entry]
CANADA
CANADA--COMMERCE
CANADA--SURVEYS
Canada.  Bilingual IFR Communications Simulation Studies
CANADA.  BUREAU OF MINES--BIBLIOGRAPHY
Canada.  Dept. of External Affairs.  Conference series, 1966
Canada.  Dept. of External Affairs
   Documents on Canadian external relations
CANADA.  DEPT. OF EXTERNAL AFFAIRS
Canada.  Dept. of External Affairs.  Academic Relations
   Division
Canada.  Royal Canadian Air Force
CANADA.  ROYAL CANADIAN AIR FORCE--BIOGRAPHY
CANADA.  ROYAL CANADIAN AIR FORCE--SEARCH AND RESCUE
   OPERATIONS
Canada.  Royal Canadian Air Force.  Concert Band
```

1/Form subheadings were used with personal names prior to AACR 1. If
special treatment is desired for these headings, see the Appendix.

7.3.   Subject Entries for Uniform Title Fields

A field representing a work about a uniform title is placed after the main and added entries for all editions of the same uniform title in the original language and translations. A subject entry about the complete uniform title precedes all main, added, and subject entries for parts of the uniform title.

Examples

```
Dante Alighieri, 1265-1321        [These uniform titles all
  Divina commedia                    begin with the heading
  Divina commedia.  English.         for Dante]
  Divina commedia.  Spanish.
  DIVINA COMMEDIA
  DIVINA COMMEDIA--CONCORDANCES
  Divina commedia.  Inferno
  Divina commedia.  Inferno.  Portuguese
  DIVINA COMMEDIA.  INFERNO

Bible.  Spanish.  Reina-Valera.  1977
BIBLE.  SPANISH--HISTORY
Bible.  Swedish.  Charles XII's Bible.  186-?
BIBLE.  SWEDISH--VERSIONS
Bible.  Welsh.  1717
BIBLE--ANTIQUITIES
BIBLE--THEOLOGY
Bible.  N.T.  Polish.  1953
Bible.  N.T.  Vietnamese.  1957
BIBLE.  N.T.--BIOGRAPHY
BIBLE.  N.T.--THEOLOGY
Bible.  N.T.  Acts.  English.  Jerusalem Bible.  1978
BIBLE.  N.T.  ACTS--COMMENTARIES
```

8.   <u>Subarrangement of Identical Fields That Have the Same Function</u>

   When the first fields of two or more filing entries represent the same entity and they are functionally identical, the entries are arranged according to their subordinate fields. The selection of subordinate fields for a filing entry must conform to one of five basic patterns:

   a.   Type 1:   (1) Main or added entry for a person or corporate body [Note that if the filing entry begins with an added entry, the main entry is <u>not</u> included as a subordinate filing field]

             (2) Title

             (3) Date of publication, distribution, etc.

   b.   Type 2:   (1) Name-title added entry

             (2) Date of publication, distribution, etc.

   c.   Type 3:   (1) Main or added entry under title

             (2) Date of publication, distribution, etc.

   d.   Type 4:   (1) Subject or series added entry (includes name-title entries and series numeration)

             (2) All fields of Type 1 or Type 3 filing entry for main entry of catalog record in question

   e.   Type 5:   (1) Established heading (on authority card) or field being referred from (in cross reference)

             (2) Heading being referred to (in see or see-also reference)

See Rule 19.2.2 for exception to Rule 8 for musical works.

41

8.1.   Choice of Title

Filing entries of Types 1, 2, 3 can contain only one title. For Type 1 entries involving a main entry, if more than one kind of title is present, the order of preference is 1) uniform title; 2) romanized title; 3) bibliographic title. For Type 1 entries involving an added entry, the order of preference is 1) romanized title; 2) bibliographic title. In the case of a Type 2 or 3 filing entry, the title to be used occurs as part of the first field.

Examples

[FILING TYPES 1, 2, 4]

```
Shaw, George Bernard, 1856-1950
  Arms and the man.  1913
Shaw, George Bernard, 1856-1950
  Arms and the man.  1958
Shaw, George Bernard, 1856-1950
  Arms and the man.  Chinese
Shaw, George Bernard, 1856-1950
  Arms and the man.  French
SHAW, GEORGE BERNARD, 1856-1950.  ARMS AND THE MAN
  Alexander, Nigel
    A critical commentary on ... 'Arms and the man'
SHAW, GEORGE BERNARD, 1856-1950.  ARMS AND THE MAN
  Carrington, Norman Thomas
    G. Bernard Shaw:  Arms and the man
Shaw, George Bernard, 1856-1950
  Caesar and Cleopatra.  1913.
Shaw, George Bernard, 1856-1950.  Caesar and Cleopatra.  1934
  [main entry under Ketchum; ignored in filing]
Shaw, George Bernard, 1856-1950
  Caesar and Cleopatra.  1952
SHAW, GEORGE BERNARD, 1856-1950.  CAESAR AND CLEOPATRA
  Deans, Marjorie
    Meeting at the Sphinx
Shaw, George Bernard, 1856-1950
  Do we agree?
    [main entry under Chesterton]
```

Shaw, George Bernard, 1856-1950
  The dying tongue of great Elizabeth
Shaw, George Bernard, 1856-1950
  Ellen Terry and Bernard Shaw
    [main entry under Terry]
Shaw, George Bernard, 1856-1950
  Essays. 1971.   [Collective uniform title]
Shaw, George Bernard, 1856-1950
  Forecasts of the coming century
    [main entry under Carpenter]
Shaw, George Bernard, 1856-1950
  Die heilige Johanna, see his Saint Joan. German.   1971.
Shaw, George Bernard, 1856-1950
  Le héros et le soldat, see his Arms and the man. French
Shaw, George Bernard, 1856-1950
  On language
Shaw, George Bernard, 1856-1950
  Saint Joan. 1924
Shaw, George Bernard, 1856-1950. Saint Joan. 1964
    [main entry under Swander]
Shaw, George Bernard, 1856-1950
  Saint Joan. 1971
Shaw, George Bernard, 1856-1950
  Saint Joan. German. 1967
Shaw, George Bernard, 1856-1950
  Selected works. 1956   [Collective uniform title]
Shaw, George Bernard, 1856-1950
  Selected works. Russ. 1946   [Collective uniform title]
Shaw, George Bernard, 1856-1950
  Selections. 1949   [Collective uniform title]
Shaw, George Bernard, 1856-1950
  Works   [Collective uniform title]
Shaw, George Bernard, 1856-1950
  Yin hsiung yü mei jen, see his Arms and the man. Chinese
Shaw, George Bernard, 1856-1950
  You never can tell. 1906
SHAW, GEORGE BERNARD, 1856-1950
  Adams, Ruth
    What Shaw really said
SHAW, GEORGE BERNARD, 1856-1950
  Braybrooke, Patrick, 1894-
    The subtlety of George Bernard Shaw

SHAW, GEORGE BERNARD, 1856-1950
  Minney, Rubeigh James, 1895-
    The bogus image of Bernard Shaw
SHAW, GEORGE BERNARD, 1856-1950
  Minney, Rubeigh James, 1895-
    Recollections of George Bernard Shaw
SHAW, GEORGE BERNARD, 1856-1950
  The wit and world of George Bernard Shaw
    [main entry under title]

[FILING TYPE 3]

The light. 1856   [monograph; main entry under Hurley]
Light. 1890   [serial]
The light. 1907   [monograph; main entry under Miller]
The light. 1909   [serial]
Light. 1923   [serial]
Light. 1930   [monograph; main entry under Rutherford]
The light. 1938   [serial; main entry under another title]
Light. 1942   [monograph; main entry under Strong]
The light. 1943   [monograph; main entry under Young]
The light. 1958   [monograph; main entry under Saint-Marcoux]
Light. 1965   [monograph; main entry under Hunt]
Light. 1968   [monograph; main entry under Waller]
Light. 1973   [serial]
Light (Braille Institute of America)   [made-up serial]

[FILING TYPES 3, 5]

Chanson de Roland
  Search also under
    Pseudo-Turpin
    Roland à Saragosse
Chanson de Roland. 1878
Chanson de Roland. 1907   [main entry under Ystorya de Carlo
                             Magno]
Chanson de Roland. 1957
Chanson de Roland. 1960   [main entry under Clark]
Chanson de Roland. 1971
Chanson de Roland. 1973   [main entry under Roncesvalles
                             (Chanson de geste)]
Chanson de Roland. 1974
Chanson de Roland. Dutch & Old French. 1977
Chanson de Roland. English. 1972
Chanson de Roland. Spanish & Old French. 1975

44

CHESS
  see also Checkmate (Chess)
             Chess players, Rating of
             Chessmen
             King (Chess)
CHESS
  Abrahams, Gerald, 1907–
    The chess mind
CHESS
  Abrahams, Gerald, 1907–
    Technique in chess
CHESS
  Academie universelle des jeux
    [main entry under title]
CHESS
  Agnel, Hyacinth R., 1799–1871
    The book of chess
CHESS
  Agostini, Orfeu Gilberto d'
    Xadrez básico
CHESS
  Alatortsev, Vladimir Alekseevich
    Problemy sovremennoĭ teoriĭ shakhmat
      [romanized title]
CHESS
  Alatortsev, Vladimir Alekseevich
    Vzaimodeistvie figur i peshek
      [romanized title]

[FILING TYPE 4]

The Literature of death and dying   [series added entry]
  Alden, Timothy, 1771–1839   [main entry]
    A collection of American epitaphs...
The Literature of death and dying
  Death and the visual arts   [title main entry]
The Literature of death and dying
  Maeterlinck, Maurice, 1862–1949
    Before the great silence

9.   Treatment of Identical Filing Entries

When two or more filing entries are identical, no effort need be made to arrange them within their group. In a manual file, the new entry can simply be placed after those already there. This situation occurs most commonly with filing entries for titles of various kinds (see Type 3 filing entry in Rule 8)

Example

```
Light (Motion picture) 1957
Light (Motion picture) 1965
Light (Motion picture) 1968
Light (Motion picture) 1969
Light (Motion picture) 1969
Light (Motion picture) 1969
```

SPECIAL RULES

10.   <u>Abbreviations</u>

Abbreviations are arranged exactly as written.

<u>Examples</u>

    M. Flip ignorait sa mort
    Madame Lynch y Solano López
    Messieurs les Anglais
    Messrs. Ives of Bridgeport
    Mister Doctor Blo
    Mistress Branican
    Mlado jutro
    M'Liss and Louie
    MM. Poule, Laigre & cie à la guerre
    Mme. Begué and her recipes
    Monsieur Butterfly
    Moon meal
    Mr. Drackle and his dragons
    Mrs. Appleyard's family kitchen
    Mrstík, Alois, 1861-1925

    Saint, Prem K.
    Saint Agnes School, Loudonville, N.Y.
    Saint-Ailme, Michel
    Saint Mary's Parish (Hagerstown, Md.)
    Saint-Paul, Yves

    Sainte-Anne-de-Sorel, Québec
    Sainte-Beuve, Charles Augustin, 1804-1869
    San Francisco Bay guardian
    Society for Analytical Chemistry
    St. Augustine (Fla.)
    St. Petersburg (Fla.)
    Ste. Genevieve Co., Mo.
    Stead, Peter

11.   Elements Ignored or Transposed

This rule considers simple cases in which an element or word in
a field is ignored or transposed in arranging a filing entry. Complex
cases or those that fit naturally into a broader rule are treated elsewhere (see Rules 13 and 16.7.1).

11.1.   Bibliographic Title Fields

The bibliographic title field is based on a transcription from
the title page and, therefore, may not be as clearly formulated for filing
as the heading fields constructed by the cataloger. Consequently, special
care should be taken when using the bibliographic title to arrange catalog
records.

The bibliographic title field is the only field in which data
elements are regularly omitted from the filing entry. The title proper
is the portion of the bibliographic title used in the filing entry. Other
title information, or subtitles, general material designations, and statements of responsibility are omitted from the filing entry. In the
examples below, the title proper is indicated by underlining.

Examples

La bibliographie en Belgique, 1967 = De bibliographie in
    België, 1967 / J. van Hove.
Bonds between atoms.
Breathless [motion picture] = A bout de souffle
Elements of speech, and Discourse concerning time / by
    William Holder; with a new introd., R. W. Rieber &
    Jeffrey L. Wollock.

The exuberant years : a guide for junior high leaders /
    Ginny Ward Holderness.
Famous overtures [sound recording] / Offenbach
Kommunikation / Joachim Holder.
Lord Macaulay's essays ; and, Lays of ancient Rome
Marcel Marceau, ou, L'art du mime
Microbiology abstracts. Section A: Industrial & applied
    microbiology.

11.2.   Bracketed Data

Bracketed data may appear occasionally in bibliographic title

fields and rarely in heading fields. If the data in brackets is the word

'sic' (which indicates an obvious mispelled word or inaccuracy), the

bracketed word is omitted from the filing entry. If the data in brackets

begins 'i.e.' (which indicates an alternative form), the data in the

brackets is omitted from the filing entry. However, if the data in brack-

ets is not 'sic' or 'i.e. ...', the data is included in the filing entry.

The most common type of bracketed data to be included in the filing entry

is a cataloger-supplied description of title page symbols that cannot be

reproduced by the available typography.

Examples

    [Chart for Tender is the night]
    Directory of 10 [cent] 1847 covers
    Duo [for] violin and piano
    Homenaje al Dr. [i.e. Doctor] D. [i.e. Don] Juan Regla
        Campistol
    PASCAL language mannual [sic]
    The Paul Anthony Buck [i.e. Brick] lectures
    Ungarn 1956 [i.e. nitten hundrede seksoghalvtreds]
    [Violin, piano music]

11.3.   Relators

Words that show the function of a person or corporate body in relation to a work (i.e., comp., ed., ill., joint author, tr.) or his role in a legal action (e.g., appellant, defendant, etc.) are ignored in filing. Note that the Library of Congress does not anticipate using relator terms in most AACR 2 cataloging.

Examples

           Lang, Andrew, 1844-1912
             Adventures among books
           Lang, Andrew, 1844-1912, ed.
             The Arabian nights entertainments
               [main entry under Arabian nights]
           Lang, Andrew, 1844-1912
             Ban and arrière ban
           Lang, Andrew, 1844-1912, ed.
             The blue fairy book
               [editor as main entry]
           Lang, Andrew, 1844-1912
             The book of dreams and ghosts
           Lang, Andrew, 1844-1912, tr.
             The Homeric hymns
               [main entry under Homerus]
           Lang, Andrew, 1844-1912, joint author
             The King over the water
               [main entry under Shield]
           Lang, Andrew, 1844-1912, ed.
             The lilac fairy book
           Lang, Andrew, 1844-1912
             Tales of Troy and Greece

           Standard Oil Company
             Background data on 100 octane gasoline
           Standard Oil Company
             The Big deep (Motion picture)
               [main entry under title]
           Standard Oil Company
             Denials of justice

```
Standard Oil Company
   Digest of laws ...
      [main entry under Palmer]
Standard Oil Company, defendant
   In the Supreme Court of Ohio
      [main entry under Ohio, plaintiff]
Standard Oil Company, appellant
   Standard Oil Company of New Jersey ...
      [main entry under Johnson]
Standard Oil Company, respondent
   The United States, petitioner ...
      [main entry under U.S. Dept. of Justice]
Standard Oil Company
   Whose oil is it?
```

11.4.   Series Entries

If a series added entry includes an ISSN, the ISSN is omitted

from the filing entry.

<u>Example</u>

```
Library research news; v. 2, no. 4
Library research news; v. 2, no. 6
Library research news; v. 3, no. 3  ISSN 0024-9270
Library research news; v. 4, no. 3  ISSN 0024-9270
Library research news, ISSN 0024-9270 ; v. 4, no. 6 [made-up]
```

11.5.   Terms of Honor and Address^{1/}

British titles of honor (Dame, Lady, Lord, Sir) and the terms of address for a married woman (e.g., Mrs.) that precede a forename in a personal name field are treated as if they followed all of the forenames in that field.

Example

```
Reynolds, John Phillips, 1863-
Reynolds, Sir John Russell, bart., 1828-1896
Reynolds, Joseph, d. 1872
Reynolds, Joseph William, 1821-1899
Reynolds, Sir Joshua, 1723-1792
Reynolds, Joshua Paul, 1906-
```

1/Rule 11.5 will not be needed at the Library of Congress, because the current LC cataloging policy is to place all terms of honor and address following the forenames, (e.g., Reynolds, Joshua, Sir, 1723-1792).

12. <u>Hyphenated Words</u>

Words connected by a hyphen are always treated as separate words. This rule applies even when the first part of a hyphenated word is a prefix that sometimes appears as an integral part of a word. This rule also applies to compound surnames.

<u>Examples</u>

        Anti-aircraft guns
        Anti-"black" magic
        The Anti-masonic Herald
        The Anti-slavery examiner
        Anti-tank weapons
        Anticaglia, Elizabeth, 1939-
        Antimasonic Party
        The antislavery origins of the Fourteenth Amendment
        Antitank warfare

        Inter
        Inter-act
        Inter-Church Committee on Chile
        Inter France quotidiens
        Inter/media
        Intera Environmental Consultants
        InterAfrican Committee for Hydraulic Studies
        Interbasin ground-water flow in southern Nevada
        Interchurch Language School
        Intermetropolitan relationsips

        Smith, Zay N.
        Smith and Jones
        Smith Barry, Robert, 1886-1949
        Smith Bros. Bluegrass Orchestra
        Smith-Burnett, G. C. K.
        Smith County Historical Society
        Smith-Hinds, William L., 1938-
        Smith Island and the Cape Fear Peninsula
        Smith Monzón, Esteban, 1883-1947
        Smith-Vaniz, William F
        Smitham, Fanny

53

13.   Initial Articles[1]

Initial articles in the nominative case are generally ignored at the beginning of a field whether they appear separately or are elided.

Table 1 lists definite and indefinite articles in various languages, in the nominative case only, which should be disregarded whenever they occur as the initial word of a title. In languages having an indefinite article, the word or words representing the cardinal numeral "one" also are given if the same form is used as an indefinite article. An initial numeral, whether used as a noun or an adjective, must always be regarded in filing. Note that there are no articles, either definite or indefinite, to be disregarded in filing in Albanian, Bulgarian, Czech, Estonian, Finnish, Latin, Latvian, Lithuanian, Polish, Russian, Serbo-Croatian, Slovak, Slovenian, Ukrainian, and most Indic languages.

Examples

    Radio!
    La radio al servicio del pueblo
    El radio-amador en las vias del mundo
    The radio amateur
    Le radio-amateur dans le monde entier

[1]In 1979, the Library of Congress adopted the cataloging policy of omitting initial articles in heading fields whenever the intent is not to file on the articles. Consequently, this rule will be applied most often for bibliographic titles.

Radio astronomy and cosmology
La radio avanza
Das Radio-Baubuch
Radio beams
The Radio City Music Hall book
Les Radio-clubs du Niger
La Radio-cristallographie
Der Radio-detektiv

Enfant, Édouard L'   [reference]
L'enfant à la découverte de l'espace
Enfant chéri des dames
L'enfant créateur de spectacle
Un Enfant d'Afrique
Enfants d'Afrique noire

TABLE 1: INITIAL ARTICLES TO BE DISREGARDED IN FILING

The following table lists definite and indefinite articles which should be disregarded according to the rule for initial articles (Rule 13). Under each language, articles in the nominative case only are listed in the following order: Singular--masculine, feminine, neuter; Plural-- same; an elided form follows its corresponding word or group of words; each article is listed only once under each language. The words in parentheses are variant forms. An asterisk (*) before an indefinite article indicates that the same form is also used for the cardinal numeral "one"; therefore, care must be taken to distinguish the meaning (see Rule 13.3).

Language	Definite Article	Indefinite Article
Afrikaans	Die	'n
Arabic	al-, el-[1]	None
Basque	See footnote 2	*Bat
Catalan	El, En,[3] L', La, Els, Les	*Un, *Una

[1]/The Arabic articles "al-" or "el-" (or the assimilated forms "ad-, ag-, ak-, an-, ar-, as-, at-, az-", if used) as initial words of a title, though joined by a hyphen to the word following, are to be disregarded in filing.

[2]/The definite article is added as a suffix to the word it makes definite.

[3]/The word "En" is used as an article in Catalan only before proper nouns beginning with a consonant.

Language	Definite Article	Indefinite Article
Danish	Den, Det, De	*En, *Et
Dutch	De, Het, 't, 's	*Een, *Eene, 'n
English	The	A, An
Esperanto	La	None
French	Le, La, L', Les	*Un, *Une
German	Der, Die, Das	*Ein, *Eine
Greek, Modern	Ho, Hē, To, Hoi, Hai, Ta, Tō	*Henas (Heis), *Mia, *Hena (Hen)
Hawaiian	Ka, Ke, Na, O 4/	He
Hebrew	ha-, he- 5/	None
Hungarian	A, Az	*Egy
Icelandic, Modern	Hinn, Hin, Hið, Hinir, Hinar	None
Irish (Gaelic)	An, An t- 6/, Na, Na h- 6/	None
Italian	Il, Lo, L', La, Gli, Gl', I, Le	Un, *Uno, *Una, Un'

4/ In Hawaiian, the "O emphatic" must be carefully distinguished from the preposition "o" and from its use as a noun, verb, adverb and conjunction.

5/ In Hebrew, disregard the articles "ha-" and "he-", when joined to the following word by a hyphen, if such a word begins the title.

6/ In Irish, "Na hUaighe" files as "Uaighe"; the same treatment applies to "An t-".

Language	Definite Article	Indefinite Article
Norwegian (Bokmål)	Den, Det, De	*En, *Et
Norwegian (Nynorsk)	Den, Det, Dei	*Ein, *Ei, *Eit
Portuguese	O, A, [7] Os, As [7]	*Um, *Uma
Provençal, Modern	Lo, Lou, Le, La, L', Li, Lis, Lu, Los, Las, Les	*Un, *Uno, *Una
Romanian	See footnote 2	*Un, *Una, *O
Spanish	El, La, Lo, [8] Los, Las	*Un, *Una
Swedish	Den, Det, De	*En, *Ett
Turkish, New	None	*Bir
Welsh	Y, Yr	None
Yiddish	Der, Di, Die, Dos	A, An, *Ein, *Eine, *Eyn, *Eyne

7/In Portuguese, the words "à" and "às" with accents are not articles and must be regarded in filing.

8/The use of the word "Lo" in Spanish as an article is very restricted and therefore must be carefully distinguished from its other uses.

13.1.   Initial Articles in Place Names and Personal Names

Initial articles that form an integral part of place names and personal names (including nicknames, sobriquets, and phrases characterizing persons) are generally regarded in arranging fields. An exception is made for English initial articles which are ignored even when required to make names intelligible (e.g., An American; The Wash); see also Rule 13.2. [Note that on current catalog records the Library of Congress will omit initial articles that should be disregarded in filing.]

Examples

Laš, Michal
Las Animas County, Colo.
Las de Barranco
Las Heras, Antonio
Las Lomas, Calif.
Las que llegaron después
Las Vegas, 1978
Las Vergnas, Raymond, 1902-
Lasa, Amaia
Lasalle, Peter
L'Enfant, Edouard

El, Eliyahu Pat-   [reference]
El   [title]
El-Ad, Avri, 1925-
El Alamein (Motion picture)
El Astillero, Spain
el-Ayouty, Eisha Yassin Mohamed, 1932-
El-Baz, Edgard, 1937-
El-Baz, Farouk
el-Boghdady, Fathalla
El Cid Campeador
El Curioso parlante   [reference]
The El Dorado Trail   [title]
El, ella y el otro
el Fathaly, Omar I.

The El Greco puzzle
El in the Ugaritic texts
el-Mokadem, Ahmed Mohamed

Ŭn, Chong-gī, 1940-
Ŭn, Hyo-gi
L'un
The un-Americans
Un de la résistance   [title]
Un des élèves de M. l'abbé Rive   [reference]
Un Français
  Vers un meilleur avenir
    [main entry under title]
Un Français
  Le vote des femmes ...   [reference]
Un kā khayāl   [title]
Un mundo   [title]
Un Tal, pseud.   [reference]

Americadomina
An American
   1776-1876
     [main entry under title]
An American
   The amazing American
     [main entry under title]
An American
   Constantinople and its environs   [reference]
An American, tr.
   History of the Spanish inquisition
     [main entry under Llorente]
An American, pseud. 1/
   Alabama claims
     [main entry under title]
American, pseud. 1/
   A journal of a tour of Italy ...   [reference]
The American   [title]
American Academy for Jewish Research

1/The Library of Congress began using "American" instead of "An American"
in 1979.

13.2.   Initial Articles in Corporate Names and Topical Subject Headings

Articles at the beginning of a field containing a corporate name or topical subject heading are disregarded in arranging entries. Articles elsewhere in such a field are considered in filing even when they come at the beginning of an element. Topical subject headings with inverted initial articles are treated like other inverted subject headings (see Rule 5.7). [Note that on current catalog records the Library of Congress will omit initial articles that should be disregarded in filing.]

Examples

Cluain Éanna arís
The Club, London   [reference]
The Club, New Haven
The Club, Rochester, N.Y.
A club. 1914.   [title]
The club. 1932   [title]
Club. 1950   [title]
Club. 1955   [title]
The club. 1957   [title]
Der Club. 1969   [title]
Club 21, New York   [reference]
The Club 1943   [corporate name]
Club accounts   [title]

Florence.   Kunsthistorisches Institut
Florence.   La Badia (Abbatia S. Mariae)
Florence.   La Nazione   [reference]
Florence.   Le Stinche
Florence.   L'Espressionismo, 1964
Florence.   Liceo scientifico Leonardo da Vinci
Florence.   L'Italica   [reference]
Florence.   Lo Sprone (Gallery)   [reference]
Florence.   Maggio musicale fiorentino

```
Starvation
State, Act of                                    [reference]
State, Communist                                 [reference]
State, Corporate                                 [reference]
State, Heads of                                  [reference]
State, Matter of                                 [reference]
State, The
State aid to education
```

13.3.   Articles Not in the Nominative Case and Words Resembling Articles

In applying Rule 13 care must be taken to identify articles that are not in the nominative case and words resembling articles. These parts of speech are regarded in filing (see examples under Rule 13.1). [An extended treatment of these pitfalls would be desirable in a filing manual.]

14.   Initials and Acronyms

Initials separated by marks of punctuation and/or spaces are treated as separate words. Acronyms and initials not separated in any way are treated as single words regardless of capitalization.

14.1.   Initials for Personal and Corporate Names

Initials that stand for the names of real or pseudonymous persons or the names of corporate bodies are arranged according to the same filing patterns and logical groups as fuller names of the same type; they are grouped before titles using the same initials.

14.2.   Initials Followed by Marks of Omission

When an initial is followed only by an ellipsis or other marks of omission, the marks are disregarded. If an additional letter or letters follows the marks of omission, they are treated as if they constitute a new word. Thus, in this case, the marks of omission are considered to be equivalent to a single space.

Examples

```
"A."
*  A  *, tr.
*A*, tr.
A***, comte d'
"A", Dr.                    [reference]
A*****, Major, pseud.
A, Mr.
A., A.
A------, A                  [reference]
A., B., ed.
```

63

```
A ..., D. G. de.
A*, E*, tr.
A., Salvador Cardenal          [reference]
a                              [title]
A:.A:. (Order)
A... a... a... kotki dwa
A. Alli Majang                 [reference:  forename/surname]
A. B. C., 1648-1714            [reference]
L'A, B, C ...
A.B.C. atlas of Isle of Wight
The A-B-C-D of successful college writing
A. B. E. M.                    [reference to corporate name]
The A.B. Gray report
A bâtons rompus
A. G., visconde de
A—g., E.
A.G.                           [reference to corporate name]
A.-G. Chemie                   [title]
"A. G.'s" Book of the rifle
A gauche de la barricade
A i u e o                      [title]
A - istov, Petr
A och O för ombud
A—ov, P G
A.R.E.A.                       [reference to corporate name]
A und O
A. V.                          [forename/surname]
A-v, Al
A—v, N.
A.V.C. fairy tales
Aa, Pieter van der, 1659-1733
AA., BB. AA. e B. C.
AB circuit breakers
The AB-Z of winemaking
AbaG, pseud
ABC                            [title]
ABC der schwachen Verben
ABC, Madrid                    [corporate name]
Abc of ocean liners
ABCDeFOBI
ABE                            [reference to corporate name]
Abem                           [corporate name]
```

```
ABGIIA                              [title]
ACME                                [reference to corporate name]
Acme Code Company
ACTH                                [title]
ACTION                              [corporate name]
Action Group                        [corporate name]
Adefa                               [corporate name]
ADLIB                               [title]
Aid for federally affected schools
AMA book of employment forms
Amherst College
ANA-AAAA Interchange                [reference to corporate name]
APICS bibliography
```

15.   Names with Prefixes

A prefix that is part of the name of a person or place is
treated as a separate word unless it is joined to the rest of the name
directly or by an apostrophe without a space. (This treatment of apostrophes is consistent with Rule 20.)

Examples

```
        Darby, Joseph R.
        D'Arcy, Paula, 1947-
        De, S.C.
        De Andrea, John, 1941-
        De Kleine aarde
        De La Cruz, Jessie Lopez, 1919-
        De Lange, Elaine
        De.P.Ca                                [reference]
        DeAndrea, William L.
        D'Ébneth, María Scholten de            [reference]
        DeBusk-Weaver Family (Musical group)
        Deformation of solids
        Del Balzo, Giulio
        DeLaurier, William J.
        Dell, Catherine
        Della brevita` della vita
        Della-Piana, Gabriel Mario, 1926-
        Della Pietra, Laura
        Dellagiovanna, Emil, 1909-
        Dell'Ara, Mario
        D'Entremont, John, 1950-
        DePaola, Helena
        Dos Santos, Hélène
        Dose, Gerd, 1942-
        Dracula
        Du Bouleau, le compte
        Du Merle, Paul
        DuBois, B.M.
        Dumas, Alexandre, 1802-1870
```

MacBride, Maud Gonne
Macdonnell, Arthur Anthony, 1854-1930
Mackay, John Henry, 1864-1933
MacNeice, Louis, 1907-1963
Marshall, Catherine, 1914-
McBirnie, William Steurt, 1920-
McCarthy, Joseph, 1908-1957
McFarland, James William, 1923-

16.   Numerals

Numbers expressed in digits or other notation (e.g., roman
numerals) precede letters and, with few exceptions (Rule 16.4 and 16.6),
they are arranged according to their numerical value (see also Rule 1.2).
As stated in Rule 11.2, a numeral in a bibliographic title may be followed
by bracketed data that is not included in the filing entry. The following rules govern the specific arrangement of numerals within their own
group.

16.1.   Punctuation in Numerals

Punctuation used to increase the readability of a numeral is
treated as if it did not exist. Punctuation used in other ways (e.g.,
decimals; separation of numerals) is treated as a space (see also Rule
16.5 for treatment of decimals). For example, 1,000 is equivalent to
1000, but 1948/1949 is equivalent to 1948 1949.

16.1.1.   Variation in Punctuation of Numerals

Punctuation of numerals depends on national usage. Although a
comma is generally used for readability and a period to introduce a decimal, the meaning of these marks of punctuation may be reversed in particular cases. Care should be taken to determine the function of a punctuation mark before deciding how it is to be treated in filing.

16.2.   Numerals in Nonarabic Notation

Numerals in nonarabic notation are interfiled with their arabic equivalents (e.g., XX is treated like 20). In the absence of any specific indication, such numerals are treated as cardinal numerals.

16.3.   Ordinal Numerals

An ordinal numeral files immediately after the cardinal numeral of the same value (i.e., 8, 8th, 9, 9th, etc.). Note, however, the treatment of an ordinal numeral in a chronological subdivision of a subject heading in Rule 16.7. When ordinality is indicated by a period after a numeral (e.g., 18. to convey 18th in German, it is interfiled with cardinal numerals.

16.4.   Fractions

A fraction is arranged as if the numeral above or to the left of the line (i.e., numerator) and the numeral below or to the right of the line (i.e., denominator) were separate numerals. In arranging fractions, the numerator is considered first (e.g., 1/2 and $\frac{1}{2}$ are treated as if they were 1 2). Fractions combined with whole numbers are considered to be separate from them even if there is no space between the whole numeral and the fraction.

16.5. Decimals

Numerals after a decimal point are arranged digit by digit, one place at a time. Decimal numerals that are not combined with a whole numal (e.g., .45) are arranged before the numeral "1". Decimal numerals that are combined with a whole numeral are arranged after all entries with the same whole numeral alone.

16.6. Subscript and Superscript Numerals

Subscript and superscript numerals are treated like separate whole numbers if they are associated with numerals (e.g., 10^6 is treated as if it were 10 6). When subscript and superscript numerals are associated with letters, they are considered part of the same word (e.g., H_2O is treated as if it were H20).

Examples

```
.300 Vickers machine gun mechanism made easy
.303 -inch machine guns and small arms
'.45-70' rifles
1:0 für Dich
1 2 3 for Christmas
The 1-2-3 guide to libraries
Het 1, 2, 3 van de economie
1, 2, 3's
1, 2, buckle my shoe
1/3 of an inch of French bread
1,3-shifts
1-4-5 boogie woogie
1/4 fambá y 19 cuentos más
1/10th hours of 48 hours a week pay roll wage calculator
$1 contest library series
1¢ life
1 uit 7
```

#1 World Way
1-Y's for mental reasons
1^{a} [i.e. Prima] Mostra Toscena/scultura
1er [i.e. Premier] Congress mondial ...
2   [title]
2 1/2 minute talk treasury
2^{6} is 64   [made-up title]
II-VI semiconducting compounds
2 anni dopo
The $2 window on Wall Street
Le 2^{e} plan Beveridge
003 1/2   [title]
3 1/2 monate Fabrik-arbeiterin
3/3's
3/4 for 3
3-5-7 minute talks on Freemasonry
3:10 to Yuma
3 and 30 watchbirds
3 a's: art, applied art, architecture
3-D scale drawing
3 died variously
3 point 2 and what goes with it
3 vo 365
3.1416 and all that
The 3.2 beer law ...
3M Company
The 3rd David Cargill lecture, 1970
The 3r's and the new religion
4-3-3 systeem
4-19-69, pseud.
4 cuentos
Die 4 Elemente
IV fireworks
4-H Club conservation activities
4H/1P, music for piano
LA IVme race
5 1/2: reflections on an age
5:5
The 5"/38 gun
5 against the house
5 BX plan for physical fitness
5-M Co.
5A and 5B
6, 5, 4, 3, 2, 1

```
5,000- and 10,000-year star catalogs
The 5000 and the power tangle
5.000 años de historia
The 5,000 fingers of Dr. T
5000 Jahre Bier
5.000 kilomètres dans le sud
$5,000 reward; or, The missing bride
```

16.7.   Dates in a Chronological File

In a chronological file (e.g., period subdivisions under the name of a place as subject; personal name with date) dates are arranged according to proper chronology so that B.C. dates precede A.D. dates in inverse numerical order. When a B.C. date occurs in other situations, however, it is treated like any other whole number. Within a chronological file, if two filing entries include a date span each of which begins with the same date, the entry which represents the shorter time span is filed first.

16.7.1.   Incompletely Expressed Dates

A historic time period that is generalized or expressed only in words is treated as if it consisted of the full range of dates for the period. For example, 16th century is arranged as 1500-1599[1] . A period subdivision in the form of "To [date]" is treated as if it were 0-[date]

[1]/A century is treated as beginning in the zero year (i.e., 1500), because most people think of centuries in this way, and not according to the technical definition which begins in the first year (i.e., 1501).

(e.g., To 1517 is arranged as 0-1517). Period subdivisions are arranged chronologically even when the dates do not appear as the first word in the subdivision. Although geologic time periods are considered to be period subdivisions when applying Rule 5.8, the geologic subdivisions are arranged alphabetically. An open-ended date in a period subdivision is arranged after subdivisions with ending dates.

Examples

United States--Foreign Relations--Revolution, 1775-1783
United States--Foreign Relations--1783-1865
United States--Foreign Relations--1789-1797
United States--Foreign Relations--Constitutional Period, 1789-1809

Egypt--History--To 332 B.C.   [0-332 B.C.]
Egypt--History--To 640 A.D.   [0-640 A.D.]
Egypt--History--332-30 B.C.
Egypt--History--Graeco-Roman period, 332 B.C.-640 A.D.
Egypt--History--30 B.C.-640 A.D.
Egypt--History--640-1250
Egypt--History--640-1882
Egypt--History--French occupation, 1798-1801
Egypt--History--1798-

India--History--To 324 B.C.   [0-324 B.C.]
India--History--324 B.C.-1000 A.D.
India--History--1000-1526
India--History--1500-1765
India--History--18th century   [1700-1799]
India--History--British occupation, 1765-1947
India--History--Rohilla War, 1774
India--History--19th century   [1800-1899]
India--History--Mutiny, 1809

English fiction--Middle English, 1100-1500
English fiction--Early modern, 1500-1700
English fiction--18th century   [1700-1799]
English fiction--19th century   [1800-1899]
English fiction--20th century   [1900-1999]

16.7.2. Qualified Dates

In a personal name field, qualifications of dates (e.g., b., ca., d., fl., or, ?) are ignored in filing and the dates are treated like their unqualified equivalents.

Example

```
Brown, John
Brown, John, 1619?-1679                              [made-up]
Brown, John, 1619 or 20-1690                         [made-up]
Brown, John, 1696?-1742
Brown, John, 18th cent.  [1700-1799]    [information card]
Brown, John, 1715-1766
Brown, John, 1800-1859
Brown, John, b. 1817
Brown, John, 1819-1840
Brown, John, d. 1826
Brown, John, 1826-1883
Brown, John, d. 1829
Brown, John, 1847-
Brown, John, fl. 1854
Brown, John, 1878-
Brown, John, 1934-
Brown, John, 1941-
Brown, Mrs. John, 1847-1935                          [reference]
Brown, John Mason, 1900-1969
```

16.7.3.   Dates with Month and Day

Dates that include the month and day as well as year are treated as if they were in year-month-day order regardless of the actual form and the months are arranged in calendar order.

Example

        Müller, Hans, 1898-
        Müller, Hans, Apr. 20, 1900-
        Müller, Hans, Oct. 22, 1900-
        Müller, Hans, Oct. 27, 1900-
        Müller, Hans, 1900 (Nov. 25)-   [made-up]
        Müller, Hans, 1900 Dec. 25-   [made-up]
        Müller, Hans, 1902-

17.   Romanization of Letters

Letters in a filing entry are limited to letters of the English alphabet (A-Z). Nonroman characters or special letters that are to be considered in filing must be converted to this alphabet. Bibliographic titles that are entirely in a nonroman alphabet present no special filing problems because they are romanized as part of the cataloging process. Special characters that appear as part of a roman alphabet title must be romanized when the filing entry is formulated. Instructions for handling particular cases are given in Rule 17.1.

17.1.   Special Characters

Several languages that use the roman alphabet also employ special letters that have no immediately recognizable equivalents in that alphabet. The following list shows how these letters are treated.

Name of character	Character		Filing value
Greek alpha		α	a
Ligature ae	Æ	ae	ae
Greek beta		β	b
Eth		ð	d
Greek gamma		γ	g
Turkish ı		ı	i
Ligature oe	Œ	oe	oe
Thorn	Þ	þ	th

76

Examples

A.B.A.V.   [reference]
A, B and C dialogue
α-, β- and γ-spectroscopy
A. B. C.   [title]
A.-G. Chemie
α-γ directional correlation in Po^{211}
A-G-E bulletin

Thorarensen, Jakob, 1886-1972
Þórarinn Arnason, 1898-
Þórarinn Jónsson, 1901-
Thorarinsson, Benedikt Sigurður
Thorburn, Thomas, 1913-
Þórðar saga hreðu   [uniform title heading]
Thordarson, Agnes
Þorðarson, Björn, 1879-
Thoreau, Henry David, 1817-1862

77

18.　　　Signs and Symbols

Nonalphabetic signs and symbols are generally ignored in filing and the next letter or numerals are used as the basis for arrangement. Exceptions to this rule are described in Rules 18.1 and 18.2. Note also that a nonalphabetic sign that looks like a letter (e.g., x as the sign of multiplication) is filed as a letter. Subscript and superscript letters are treated like separate whole letters (e.g. L^x is treated as if it were L x). See also Rule 1.3.1 which covers the treatment of punctuation and Rule 11.2 which covers the treatment of bracketed data to represent nonprintable signs or symbols. See also examples under Rules 14.2 and 16.6

Examples

```
100 alphabets publicitaires
100% American (Motion picture)
100 anni di educazione fisica
The $100 bond news
100 chapel talks
100% cooperation with the United States
100 embalming questions answered
$100 gets you started
100% histoire d'un patriote
100 Jahre Brennerbahn
Las 100 más famosas novelas
100¢ on the dollar                            [made-up]
100 percent insurance on ship mortgage
100 pounds of popcorn
The £100 wager                                [made-up]
100 x Zeichnen und Malen
100 years an orphan

1:0 für Baby
1+1                                           [English title]
1+1 = 1                                       [English title]
1 2 3 for Christmas
1+12 = 13                                     [German title]
```

```
1 see 4                                          [title]
1 x 1 der Kunstharzpresserei
1 x 1 der Taktik
1-Y's for mental reasons


Estimating $L_x(1)$
Estimating life-cycle costs
The unveiling of Dynacamera 3                    [made-up title]
The unveiling of Dynacamera $^{TM}$2
```

18.1.   Treatment of the Ampersand

The ampersand (&) is the only symbol which has filing value. The ampersand has the lowest filing value in the alphanumeric order of characters; thus it follows spaces and precedes the lowest Arabic numeral or alphabetic character. Depending on the circumstances, the cataloger may supply a cross reference or added entry from the language equivalent of the ampersand.

<u>Example</u>

```
A. & A. Enterprises Incorporated
A & B roads & motorways atlas of Great Britain
A & H Printers
A & O Österreich
A & P cookbook and shopping guide
"A" 1-12
A 18. a cadeira
A 22 & 23
A 99, Autobahnring München
A.A.V.                                [reference]
The A.A. way of life
A. Alvarez, Roy Fuller, Anthony Thwaite
A and B roads and motorways atlas of Great Britain
A. and G. motor vehicle year book
A and H Printers                      [made-up reference]
```

```
       A and M Consolidated Independent School District
       A und O
       A und O Österreich                        [made-up reference]
```

18.2.   "Names" Consisting of Symbols[1]

When the leading element of a filing entry consists only of
symbols (e.g., *** as a pseudonym), the entry is arranged at the beginning of the file before an ampersand or the lowest numeral. Fields containing "names" of this kind are grouped in the following order:

  a.   Symbols with or without relator

  b.   Symbols with additional word(s)

  c.   Symbols with forename(s)

Within each of these groups, references beginning with a "name" in symbols are subarranged by the heading referred to, before added entries
which are subarranged by bibliographic title. Differences in the symbols
used have no bearing on the arrangement.

[1]/A name consisting of symbols is not permitted under AACR 1 or AACR 2.

80

Examples

```
****, tr.
  see Péreira da Costa, Constantino
***
  see Seton, William
***
  Die algerische Revolution
? ? ?
  Un aventurier vous parle
____?
  East and west
?
  Recollections of three kaisers
***, ed.
  Vitrine XIII
... ...?
  Zjebany nawożenja
***, abbé
***, avocat                                    [reference]
_____, Bishop of
* *
 * , Landgerichtsdirektor
* *, Mademoiselle de
**, Mr.
* *
 * , pseud.
  Der Giftbau                                  [reference]
卍, pseud.
  The language of the stars                   [reference]
* * *, U.S. Army                              [reference]
___ , James J                                [reference]
* * *, Marie
```

19. Uniform Titles

The following section deals with subarrangement of uniform title fields.

19.1. Examples Showing Subarrangement of Uniform Titles

The following examples illustrate the arrangement of entries under uniform titles as provided for in Rules 5.5.1, 7, 8, and 9. They do do not illustrate any new principles of arrangement.

Examples

```
Upanishads
  1898        [imprint date regarded; bibliographic title ignored]
Upanishads
  1912
Upanishads
  1953
Upanishads
  1953
Upanishads
  1967
Upanishads.  Bengali and Sanskrit.  Selections
  1966
Upanishads.  English
  1957
Upanishads.  English.  Selections
  1938
Upanishads.  Hindi
   1962
Upanishads.  Yiddish
  1958
UPANISHADS
  Banerjee, Hiranmay, 1905        ...
UPANISHADS
  Godel, Roger      ...
UPANISHADS
  Sharma, Vidya Sagar      ...
UPANISHADS--BIBLIOGRAPHY
```

Upanishads. Aitareyopaniṣad
   1965
Upanishads. Aitareyopaniṣad. English
   1899
Upanishads. Īsópaniṣad
   1943
Upanishads. Īsópaniṣad. English
   1968
UPANISHADS. ĪSÓPANIṢAD--CRITICISM,
   INTERPRETATION, ETC.
Upanishads. Praśnopaniṣad
   1944
Upanishads. Praśnopaniṣad. English
   1929
Upanishads. Selections
   1960
Upanishads. Taittirīyopaniṣad
   1942
Upanishads, Gītā and Bible

19.2.   Musical Works

Uniform titles for musical works include subordinate elements
that describe type of score, opus number, catalog number, medium of per-
formance, key, etc., in addition to the more common data elements used in
uniform titles to describe language, parts and versions. When different
types of subordinate elements occur in the same relative position (for
example, as the second element in the field), the fields are grouped in
the following order:

   a. Date
   b. Language
   c. Arranged statement (i.e., arr.)
   d. All other subordinate elements (e.g. form subheading,
       musical form, catalog number, medium, key)
   e. Qualifying words

19.2.1.   Treatment of "Sound recording"

When the term "Sound recording" ("Phonodisc" for many pre-
AACR 2 catalog records) is used with a uniform title, it is arranged before all other uniform title data elements occurring in the same relative
position, except the date of publication, distribution, etc.

Examples

        Beethoven, Ludwig van, 1770-1827
          [Chamber music. Selections. Sound recording]   [made-up]
          [Piano music. Selections]   [made-up]
          [Quartets, strings, no. 1-6, op. 18]
          [Quartets, strings, no. 1-6, op. 18] Phonodisc
          [Quartets, strings, no. 1-6, op. 18. Sound recording] [made-up]
          [Quartets, strings, no. 1-6, op. 18; arr]
          [Quartets, strings, no. 1-6, op. 18 (Sketches)]
          Sonata, piano, no. 4, op. 7, E$^\flat$ major. [Sound recording] 1978
          [Sonata, piano, no. 5, op. 10, no. 1, C minor]
          [Sonata, piano, no. 8, op. 13, C minor] [Sound recording]
          [Sonatas, piano, no. 1-3, op. 2, no. 1-3]
          [Sonatas, piano, no. 5-6, op. 10, no. 1-2] Phonodisc
          [Sonatas, piano, no. 5-7, op. 10] [Sound recording]
          [Sonatas, piano, no. 8, op. 13, C minor]
          [Works, chamber music. Selections] [Sound recording]
          [Works, piano. Selections]

        Mozart, Johann Chrysostom Wolfgang Amadeus, 1756-1791
          [Don Giovanni]
          [Don Giovanni. German & Italian]
          [Don Giovanni. Italian]
          [Don Giovanni; arr.]
          [Don Giovanni. Batti, batti, o bel Masetto]
          [Don Giovanni. Libretto. English]
          Don Giovanni. Overture. [Sound recording] 1976
          [Don Giovanni. Piano-vocal score. English & Italian]
          [Don Giovanni. Selections]

Telemann, Georg Philipp, 1681-1767
  The baroque art of Telemann   [reference]
  [Concerto, 2 flutes & string orchestra, A major]
  [Concerto, 2 recorders & string orchestra, B$\flat$ major]
  [Concerto, 3 oboes, 3 violins & continuo, B$\flat$ major]
  [Concerto, 3 trumpets, 2 oboes & string orchestra, D major]
  [Concerto, flute & string orchestra, G major]
  [Concerto, flute, oboe d'amore & bass, G major]
  [Concerto, oboe & string orchestra, C minor]
  [Concerto, oboe & string orchestra, F minor] Phonodisc
  [Concerto, recorder, oboe, violin & continuo solo, D major
    [Sound recording]
  Concerto in A major, Ouvertüre in D major [and] Trio in E minor [ref.]
  [Concerto polonoise, string orchestra, G major]
  [Concertos. Selections] Phonodisc
  [Fantasia, viola da gamba, D major]
  [Fantasias, harpsichord. No. 1-12] Phonodisc
  [Fantasias, harpsichord. Selections; arr.]
  [Harmonischer Gottesdienst. Deine Toten werden leben]
  [Harmonischer Gottesdienst. Selections]
  [Passion (St. Mark: 1759) German] Phonodisc
  [Passion (St. Matthew: 1730)] Phonodisc

19.2.2.   Subarrangement of Added Entries for Musical Works

An exception to Rule 8 is made for the Type 1 filing entry pattern whenever musical works are being arranged. In order to group the added entries for a musical performer in a logical way, it is necessary to subarrange by main entry, then uniform title and date.

Example

[These added entries all begin
with the heading for Rampal]

Rampal, Jean Pierre
  The art of Jean-Pierre Rampal   [title main entry]
  Bach, Carl Philipp Emanuel, 1714-1788
    [Concerto, harpsichord & string orchestra, W. 22,
       D minor; arr.] Phonodisc
  Baroque chamber music   [title main entry]
  Beethoven, Ludwig van, 1770-1827
    [Works, chamber music. Selections] [Sound recording]
  Benda, Franz, 1709-1786
    [Concerto, flute & string orchestra, E minor] Phonodisc
  Chaynes, Charles
    [Concerto, trumpet] Phonodisc
  Cimaroso, Domenico, 1749-1801
    [Concerto, 2 flutes, G major] Phonodisc
  A Concert at Schoenbrunn Palace in Vienna [title main entry]

20. Words with Apostrophes

Elided words, possessives, and other words with apostrophes are arranged as one word, disregarding the apostrophe, except as noted in Rule 20.1.

Examples

J. Reuben Clark, Jr., diplomat and statesman
Ja! Til sionismen?
J'accuse
Jack and the beanstalk
J'ai cent visages
Jeanne Damon's quick knits #1
Jeanne d'Arc et autres textes
Jean's way
J'étais un snob
Le Jeu d'amour

The do's
Dos accidentes do trabalho
Do's and don'ts for musicians
Dos and don'ts for notaries
Do's and dont's in Europe, 1954
The do's and don't's of delightful dieting
Dos and donts of radio writing
Dos devanceiros ao dezaoito

20.1. Elided Initial Articles

When the first part of the elision is an initial article in the nominative case, it is generally ignored; see Rule 13 for specific details.

AIDS TO CATALOG USE

The arrangement of entries in a large bibliographic file cannot be suitable for various types of searches and at the same time be so simple that it is self-explanatory. Regular users of a file should be familiar with the general principles of its arrangement, but it is unrealistic to expect that many of them will know the rules well enough to locate every entry without some guidance. Infrequent users are obviously in need of still more help. Thus, even the most consistent set of rules must be explained by various devices that are readily available to users. This need is especially great in the case of the present rules because the principles of arrangement differ significantly from those familiar to many users.

Types of Aids

The following aids should be provided to explain the structure of the catalog:

1. A detailed filing manual. This is a necessity for filers and frequent users of the catalog.

2. A brief version of the essential rules. This should be posted prominently at various points in the area of the card catalog, included in the user documentation for the online retrieval system, included at the beginning of each volume of printed and microform catalogs, and made available to individual users in sheet and/or card form.

3. <u>Information cards and references</u>. Three types are needed: explanatory references, specific filing references, and arrangement cards. They should be provided at appropriate points in the catalog itself. The following sections describe the content and use of each type.

Explanatory References

An explanatory reference briefly explains a particular filing rule, describes its effect on entries in variant forms, and points to other parts of the file where these entries may be found. By functioning as a general reference for a category of headings (e.g., those beginning with a numeral), an explanatory reference minimizes the need for specific filing references.

This type of catalog aid is filed with sizable groups of entries under variant forms of the same item. For example, the explanation of the treatment of numbers belongs with entries beginning with numerals and with groups of entries beginning with specific numbers expressed in words (e.g., one, one hundred).

Explanatory references should be made to explain the following rules: abbreviations, hyphenated words (file only under common prefixes); initials and acronyms (only with entries filed as separate letters); names with prefixes (file only under common prefixes); numerals. See Figure 1 for an example. The need for explanatory references for other rules would be dictated by the structure and size of a given file.

Specific Filing References

A reference should be made for a specific heading or group of headings that, by the rules, may be located in an unusual or unexpected position in the file. It is made by reconstructing the heading so that the reference can be filed in the desired alternative location where the user might be expected to look for the heading. Figure 2 gives an example of a filing reference for a group of headings. Similar references should be made for other common names whose form has changed significantly under AACR 2, e.g., forenames, place names, etc. Figure 3 exemplifies a filing reference for a single heading. Similar linking references should be made from the AACR 2 form of name to the pre-AACR 2 form of name. This type of catalog aid supplements references from alternative forms of heading required by the descriptive and subject cataloging rules.

Arrangement Cards

The arrangement of entries under certain headings (typically uniform titles and voluminous authors) may be frequently so complex that a user cannot be expected to find his way without assistance. To alleviate his problems, the arrangement of the group of entries should be described briefly on a card that is filed at the beginning of the group. In a long file (such as entries for the Bible), it may be desirable to intersperse several such cards at strategic points. Figure 4 gives an example of an arrangement card.

Figure 1.--Explanatory reference

Information Card: Treatment of Numbers

Numbers expressed as numerals (e.g., 4, 1984, XX) precede
words consisting of letters and they are arranged according to
their numerical value (roman numerals are treated like arabic
numerals).

Numbers expressed as words (e.g., four, nineteen eighty-
four, twenty) are filed alphabetically.

If you do not find what you want in this portion of the
catalog, look under the alternative form. When looking for a
verbal form, bear in mind that it will appear in the language
of the item you are seeking and that the verbal form may be
expressed in any one of several ways (e.g., one hundred, a
hundred) which file in different places in the catalog.

Figure 2.--Filing reference for a group of headings

John the ...

Under AACR 2, entries for headings beginning with a forename can generally be found in a group before the same word
used as a surname. For example, John, the Baptist files before
John, Angela V. For entries established prior to AACR 2, words
or phrases commonly associated with a forename often were not
preceded by a comma and, thus, file after the surnames. For
example, John, Ursula files before John the Prophet, Saint.
Thus, compound forenames (John Paul) and forenames without
commas (John-the-Giant-Killer) follow single surnames and are
interfiled with titles (John: the Gospel of belief).

92

Figure 3.--Filing reference for a single heading

[as it would appear for a library that begins
a new catalog for AACR 2 entries]

Australian Bureau of Statistics

For works cataloged before 1981 search

in the old catalog under

Australia. Bureau of Statistics

Figure 4.--Arrangement card

Goethe, Johann Wolfgang von, 1749-1832

    Entries under this heading are grouped as follows:
Works written, edited, or translated by the author
and works to which he contributed in some other manner
are arranged by title. Collective uniform titles* are
filed alphabetically among individual titles.
    Under each title, the groupings are as follows:
1) editions in the original language and added entries
for related works, by date; 2) works about the title,
by author, title, and date; 3) translations of the work,
by language and date.
    Works about the author follow the individual titles
and are arranged by author of the work, title, and date.

*Correspondence, Plays, Poems, Selections, Works

APPENDIX

Alternative Rules for Arrangement of Pre-AACR 2 Forms

The Library of Congress Filing Rules was written to arrange headings formulated under various cataloging rules and practices. However,
the filing rules emphasize the conventions exemplified in AACR 2 headings and the resulting arrangements reflect this emphasis. For example, in corporate headings formulated according to AACR 2 the comma
can be ignored in determining leading elements, whereas in pre-AACR 2
headings, a comma may signal a cataloger's addition to the heading and
thus may be used to determine a leading element. Nevertheless, Rule 5.4
ignores the comma in filing, resulting in an arrangement consisting of
two filing subgroups for corporate headings. This arrangement is different from one in which the comma is used to determine the leading
element; in such a case the resulting arrangement is one consisting of
three filing subgroups (cf. Rule A.2.2).

In addition to emphasizing AACR 2 conventions, the main text does
not provide special filing treatment for forms of headings that cannot
occur under AACR 2 as long as application of those rules produces
reasonable results. For example, although under ALA Rules the addition
of a form subheading to a personal name resulted in an entirely different entity (e.g., Homerus. Spurious and doubtful works), it is
possible to apply Rule 7.1 and to file such form subheadings as if they

were titles. However, in one situation it was necessary to add a special rule for pre-AACR 2 headings to the main text, namely the one for names consisting of symbols (Rule 18.2). Otherwise, the application of Rule 18 would have meant that personal names consisting entirely of symbols would have no filing value at all, since Rule 18 specifies that all symbols are ignored.

Given the conditions described above, some institutions may wish to apply the alternative rules provided in this appendix. As the previous discussion indicates, the main text is sufficient for any institution that does not need to file pre-AACR 2 forms or that has so few pre-AACR 2 forms that they do not require special filing treatment. Thus the alternative rules will not be applied at the Library of Congress because the new Add-on Catalog will contain only AACR 2 and AACR 2-compatible headings. However, this appendix has been written for those institutions that do not begin new AACR 2 catalogs in 1981 and that have a significant number of pre-AACR 2 forms to file in their catalogs. Each institution must determine for itself whether there is sufficient need to apply the alternative rules provided here.

A.1.   Personal Name Fields

When formulating personal name headings under ALA or earlier cataloging rules, it was possible to create an entirely different name by adding a form subheading (e.g., Legend; Spurious and doubtful works) to the established form of name (e.g., Shakespeare, William, 1564-1616; Shakespeare, William, 1564-1616. Spurious and doubtful works). Such names with form subheadings are arranged after all main, added, and subject entries relating to the name on which they are based. Note that if Rule A.1 is followed, it partially supersedes Rule 7.1 in the main text.

Example

```
Vergilius Maro, Publius
  Bucolica
Vergilius Maro, Publius
  Georgica
Vergilius Maro, Publius
  Two dramatizations from Vergil      [reference]
VERGILIUS MARO, PUBLIUS--CONCORDANCES
VERGILIUS MARO, PUBLIUS--TECHNIQUE
Vergilius Maro, Publius.  Spurious and doubtful works
```

A.2.   Corporate Name Fields

Corporate names established prior to AACR 2 may exhibit three characteristics not present in headings established after 1980 as follows: 1) use of the inversion technique that made the surname the entry element in those cases of corporate names beginning with one or more initials and/or forenames; 2) addition to the heading of a local place name preceded by a comma to distinguish two corporate bodies with the same name; 3) use of certain relator terms (e.g., appellant, defendant) to indicate a relationship of a legal nature between a heading and a work entered under that heading. Each of these characteristics should be given special filing treatment as described below.

A.2.1.   Corporate Names with Inverted Initials and/or Forenames

The leading element of an inverted corporate name that begins with a surname followed by initials and/or forenames ends before the mark of punctuation that indicates the inverted element. A heading of this type interfiles among headings with the same surname. The words following the inverted element up to the next period are treated as part of the inverted element. Subheadings under an inverted corporate heading (e.g., Thompson (J. Walter) Company. Market Research Dept.) are treated as separate elements. Note that if Rule A.2.1 is followed, it partially supersedes Rules 3.3.2 and 5.4 in the main text.

Examples

    Bender, Marylin
    Bender (Matthew) and Company, inc.
    Bender, Matthew F., 1906-

    Thompson, J. S. T.
    Thompson (J. Walter) Aust. Pty., ltd.
    Thompson (J. Walter) Company
    Thompson (J. Walter) Company. Market Research Dept.
    Thompson (J. Walter) Far Eastern Company
    Thompson, Jack C., 1909-

    Wilson, H. Clyde
    Wilson, H. W. Allen   [made-up]
    Wilson, H. W., firm, publishers
    Wilson, Holly Skodol

A.2.2.   Order of Subordinate Filing Elements for Corporate Name Fields

        When the leading elements of two or more corporate name fields

are identical but they are modified by different means, the fields are

grouped in the following order:

    a. Corporate name alone

    b. Corporate name followed by parenthetical qualifier

    c. Corporate name followed by a comma and additional word(s)

Subarrangement within any group is by succeeding subordinate elements.

Note that if Rule A.2.2 is followed, it supersedes Rule 5.4 in the main

text.

        Automobile Association
        Automobile Association. Publications Division
        Automobile Association (Hawkes Bay)
        Automobile Association (Wanganui)
        Automobile Association, Auckland, N.Z.
        Automobile Association, Taranaki, N.Z.   [made-up]
        Automobile Association of Ceylon

A.2.3.   Corporate Names with Legal Relators

        Words that show the role of a corporate body in a legal action
are considered in arranging fields. Names qualified in this way are
grouped after unqualified names used as main and added entries and before
the unqualified name as a subject heading. This places them also before
the unqualified name with a subheading. Note that if Rule A.2.3 is followed, it partially supersedes Rule 11.3 in the main text.

        Example

        Standard Oil Company
          Background data on 100 octane gasoline
        Standard Oil Company
          The Big deep (Motion picture)
            [main entry under title]
        Standard Oil Company
          Denials of justice
        Standard Oil Company
          Digest of laws ...
            [main entry under Palmer]
        Standard Oil Company
          Whose oil is it?
        Standard Oil Company, appellant
          Standard Oil Company of New Jersey ...
            [main entry under Johnson]
        Standard Oil Company, appellant
          Standard Oil Company of New Jersey ...
            [main entry under United States, appellee]

Standard Oil Company, defendant
  In the Supreme Court of Ohio
    [main entry under Ohio, plaintiff]
Standard Oil Company, petitioner
  The Standard Oil Company of New York ...
    [main entry under U.S. Dept. of Justice]
Standard Oil Company, respondent
  The United States, petitioner ...
    [main entry under U.S. Dept. of Justice]
STANDARD OIL COMPANY
  Baker, John Calhoun, 1895-
    Directors and their functions
Standard Oil Company. Committeee on Reservoir Development
  and Operation
  Joint progress report ...
Standard Oil Company. Marine Dept.   [reference]

A.3.   <u>Terms Indicating Medium of Material Cataloged</u>

There are significant variations in the display and use of
terms indicating the medium, or physical format, of an item being cataloged, depending on which cataloging rules and practices were in effect
at the time. Prior to AACR 2, terms indicating the medium were enclosed
either in brackets or parentheses. In all such cases, the term began
with an upper-case letter. Under AACR 2, the decision to use such terms
(called general material designations or GMDs in AACR 2) is optional.
Each institution makes three decisions in regard to GMDs: 1) which GMD
terms to use; 2) whether to include the GMD following the title proper in
the title and statement of responsibility area; 3) whether to include
the GMD at the end of the uniform title in heading fields. When the GMD
is included in the bibliographic title field, it is enclosed in brackets
and begins with a lower-case letter. When the GMD is included in
uniform titles, it is preceded by a period instead of being enclosed in
brackets and begins with an upper-case letter.

As described above, the variations both in the application of
terms indicating medium and in the forms of their display mean that each
institution must formulate its own filing policy regarding the treatment
of such terms in filing entries. The Library of Congress has decided to
omit such terms from filing entries for bibliographic titles (see
Rule 11.1) and to regard such terms whenever present in heading fields.

The practical effect of the policies described above is that different entries for the same work may vary in the presence or absence of a term indicating medium of material cataloged. Each institution must consider its own catalog, the possibility of it containing different entries for the same work in different media, and its users' needs to be aware of such differences.

One possible filing approach would be always to include and file on terms indicating the medium (see Example A). In this case, the institution may need to add GMDs to some AACR 2 added entries to allow them to interfile properly with older entries for the same work. A second filing approach would be always to exclude these terms (see Example B). In this case, the institution will need to distinguish carefully between terms for medium given in parentheses (a pre-AACR 2 practice) that are to be ignored and qualifying terms given in parentheses (AACR 2 and pre-AACR 2) that are to be regarded. A third filing approach would be to file each entry exactly as it appears (see Example C).

Example A

America: a personal history of the United States. [Motion
    picture] no. 1
America: a personal history of the United States. [Motion
    picture] no. 10
America: a personal history of the United States; no. 13
    [made-up motion picture]
America: a personal history of the United States. [Video-
    recording] no. 1
America: a personal history of the United States. [Video-
    recording] no. 10
America: a personal history of the United States; no. 13
    [made-up videorecording]

Star-spangled banner (Anglo-Saxon poem)   [made-up]
Star-Spangled Banner (Filmstrip)   1967
The Star-Spangled Banner. [Filmstrip]   1975
Star-spangled banner [filmstrip]   1985   [made-up]
Star-Spangled Banner (Motion picture)   1971
The Star-Spangled Banner. [Motion picture]   1975
Star-spangled banner (Motion picture : 1982) [made-up]

Example B

America: a personal history of the United States. [Motion
    picture] no. 1
America: a personal history of the United States. [Video-
    recording] no. 1
America: a personal history of the United States. [Motion
    picture] no. 10
America: a personal history of the United States. [Video-
    recording] no. 10
America: a personal history of the United States; no. 13
America: a personal history of the United States; no. 13

Star-Spangled Banner (Filmstrip)   1967
Star-Spangled Banner (Motion picture)   1971
The Star-Spangled Banner. [Filmstrip]   1975
The Star-Spangled Banner. [Motion picture]   1975
Star-spangled banner [filmstrip]   1985
Star-spangled banner (Anglo-Saxon poem)
Star-spangled banner (Motion picture : 1982)

Example C

America: a personal history of the United States; no. 13
America: a personal history of the United States; no. 13
America: a personal history of the United States. [Motion
  picture] no. 1
America: a personal history of the United States. [Motion
  picture] no. 10
America: a personal history of the United States. [Video-
  recording] no. 1
America: a personal history of the United States. [Video-
  recording] no. 10

Star-spangled banner (Anglo-Saxon poem)
Star-Spangled Banner (Filmstrip)   1967
The Star-Spangled Banner. [Filmstrip]   1975
Star-spangled banner [filmstrip]   1985
Star-Spangled Banner (Motion picture)   1971
The Star-Spangled Banner. [Motion picture]   1975
Star-spangled banner (Motion picture : 1982)

INDEX

References are to pages; underlining
indicates a reference to an example.

Part (of a larger work)
    and form subheadings, 31
    in bibliographic titles, 33
    in music uniform titles, 83, 84-85
    in uniform titles, 31-32, 40, 83
Period subdivisions, 34-35, 72-73
Personal names
    See also Forenames; Surnames
    arrangement by date, 72, 74, 75
    consisting of initials, letters,
        numerals or phrases, 16, 18, 24-25
    consisting of symbols, 80-81
    initial articles, 59-60
    initials for, 63-64
    leading element, 16, 17-18, 24-25
    placement, 24-25
    pre-AACR 2 forms, 97
    with form subheadings, 39, 97
    with prefixes, 66
    with relators, 50
"Phonodisc", 84, 85-86
Phrases as personal names, 16, 18,
    24-25
Place names
    initial articles, 59
    leading element, 18, 19
    placement, 24-25
    qualified, 28-29
    subordinate element order, 28-29
    with prefixes, 66
Pre-AACR 2 headings, 1, 6, 95-105
Prefixes
    explanatory references, 90
    in hyphenated words, 53
    in names, 66
Principles exemplified in filing
    rules, 4-5
Punctuation, 13
    in forename qualifiers, 26-27
    in numerals, 68, 70-72
    in terms indicating medium, 102
Punctuation, Significant and non-
    significant, 15, 18-19, 20-22,
        22-23
    definition, 10

Qualified dates, 74
Qualifying words
    See Parenthetical qualifiers

References
    See Explanatory references
        Filing references
        Linking references
        See and see also refer-
            ences
Relators, 50-51
    in corporate names, 50-51,
        100-101
    in names consisting of sym-
        bols, 80-81
    in surnames, 27
Roman numerals, 12, 69, 70-71
Romanized letters, 76
Romanized titles, 42, 45

"Saint" filing example, 47
See and see-also references
    aids to catalog use, 91
    functional order, 36-37
    subordinate fields, 41, 44,
        45
"Selections", 31-32, 82-85
Serial titles, 31, 33, 44
Series fields
    ISSN ignored, 51
    leading element, 19-20
    subordinate elements, 33
    subordinate fields, 41, 45
"Sic" as bracketed data, 49
Significant punctuation:
    definition, 10, 15

Signs and symbols, 13, 78-81
    ampersand, 79-80
    bracketed data, 49
    names consisting of, 80-81
"Sound recording", 84, 85-86
Special letters, 76-77
(Spirit) filing example, 28
"Spurious and doubtful works",
    17, 39, 95, 97

Subject entries
   functional order, 36-37
   subordinate fields, 38-39, 41-45
   uniform titles, 40
Subject subdivisions, 34-35, 38-39
Subordinate elements
   definition, 9
   order of, 26-35
Subordinate fields, Selection of,
   41-45
Subscript and superscript letters,
   78-79
Subscript and superscript numerals,
   70-71
Surnames
   See also Personal names
   compound, 17, 28, 53
   leading element, 16, 17
   placement, 24-25
   subordinate elements, 27-28
Symbols
   See Signs and Symbols

Terms indicating medium, 102-105
Terms of address for married
   women, 52
Thorn (Icelandic character), 76, 77
Titles (main or added entry)
   See also Bibliographic titles
          Romanized titles
          Uniform titles
   leading element, 20-22
   placement, 24
   subordinate fields, 33
Titles of honor, 52
"To" in period subdivisions, 72-73
Topical subdivisions, 34-35
Topical subject headings
   initial articles, 61-62
   inverted, 22, 34
   leading element, 22-23
   placement, 24, 34-35
   punctuation, 22-23
   qualified, 34
Treaty headings, 31-32
Turkish ı, 76

Uniform titles
   arrangement cards, 91, 93
   definition for filing, 19
   for musical works, 83-86
   inclusion in filing entry,
     42-45
   leading element, 19, 20
   placement, 24, 31-32, 82-83
   qualified, 31
   subordinate elements, 31-32
   subordinate fields, 41-45,
     82-83
   subject entries for, 40

Version in uniform titles, 31-
   32

Words: filing definition, 9
Words added in filing, 14
   bracketed data, 49
   dates, 72-73
Words changed in filing, 14
   nonarabic numerals, 69, 71
   nonroman letters, 76, 77
Words ignored in filing, 14
   bibliographic titles, 48-49
   bracketed data, 49
   initial articles, 54-62
   qualifications of dates, 74
   series, 51
Words transposed in filing, 14
   dates in period subdivi-
     sions, 73
   dates with month and day, 75
   terms of honor and address,
     52

☆U.S. GOVERNMENT PRINTING OFFICE: 1980 O—327-259